BUILD YOUR BUNKER!

STOP The Government Taxation
Of Your Financial Future

by
Rick Bueter

The Declaration of Independence

In CONGRESS, July 4, 1776

The unanimous Declaration of the thirteen united States of America

"When in the Course of human events it becomes necessary for one people to dissolve the political bands which have connected them with another and to assume among the powers of the earth, the separate and equal station to which the Laws of Nature and of Nature's God entitle them, a decent respect to the opinions of mankind requires that they should declare the causes which impel them to the separation.

We hold these truths to be self-evident, that all men are created equal, that they are endowed by their Creator with certain unalienable Rights, that among these are

Life, Liberty and the pursuit of Happiness."

fi•nan•cial + bun•ker

1. where the wealthiest individuals and financial institutions in America hold billions of dollars

2. one of the last protected Freedoms found in the Internal Revenue Service Tax Code

3. the last place Government will come looking for money

Build Your Bunker.

BUILD YOUR BUNKER!

STOP The Government Taxation Of Your Financial Future

First Edition 2013

Publisher's Note:

This book is intended for educational purposes only and does not provide legal, tax, or investment advice. Readers should consult a qualified professional before acting on any of the information contained herein. Any references to outside sources have been edited for clarification purposes. Information contained herein is from sources believed to be accurate but is not warranted.

The use of financial illustrations, tax rates and projections are intended for educational purposes only, actual numbers should be obtained by a qualified professional.

Go to **www.BuildYourBunker.com/HELP** to speak with a licensed professional who is an expert in building Financial Bunkers®

Published by LegacySafe Publishing

Printed in The United States of America.

First printing, November 2013 - Second Edition

ISBN 978-0-615-90790-1

LegacySafe Publishing
9820 Willowcreek Road, Suite 410
San Diego, CA 92131

(858)621-9099

Contents

About This Book

It's been three years since writing my last book The Great Wall Street Retirement Scam. When I wrote that book, I had been thinking about all of that content for several years before putting it down in writing. Since that time I have had a chance to sit back and watch the world, our Government, and the financial planning industry react to the world financially. What I have concluded is that everyone keeps doing the same things and getting the same results.

Older Americans continue to live with financial fears and worry. The working class has no confidence in the 401k retirement system and rightly so. Many families just starting out are buried in debt from education, credit cards and mortgages. Independent business people are continuing to be squeezed by more and more Government regulation. The cause of Freedom as penned in The Declaration of Independence by the Founding Fathers of America is being diluted. Freedom is being stolen and government leaders are allowing it to happen right in front of our eyes.

Please don't get me wrong. I believe that the people of our country hold greatness. However, we are losing our way. We have moved so far away from the vision of our founders that real Freedom is in jeopardy. If we cannot make change with our Government, we must make change for ourselves and prepare for the future.

I believe Freedom begins with independence.

Today independence is directly tied to money. The more independent you are of banks, Wall Street, and the Government, the more Freedom you hold in your life.

Since the creation of IRAs and 401ks, the financial planning process Americans have been presented with has made banks,

Wall Street and the Government rich at the expense of the American people. An understanding about how banks, government and Wall Street really work is absent in the typical financial planning process. The direct connection between money, and Freedom should be one of the basic principles of any financial planning discussion. From that, the answers to where money should reside become simple. If everyone in America built their financial house starting with a Financial Bunker, Americans would be empowered with more Freedom than anyone could imagine.

This book is not just about the confiscation of money, it's about the confiscation of **Freedom**. Whether you are just starting out, or are a multi-millionaire, this book will empower you with invaluable knowledge about money and what you can do with it. It's what THEY don't want you to know.

You may not be the next billionaire or have the wealth of Warren Buffet, but you don't have to be. There is a simple, yet effective way for you to win the confiscation game. **You pay income taxes once on your money, and never pay income taxes on that money again.** That is what the ultra wealthy do, and you can do it too. The goal is to create a Financial Bunker filled with as much money as possible. And when you have accomplished that, you'll have the full use, control and liquidity of that money at any point in your life, without paying any more income taxes on it. That is true Freedom. That is the Freedom of a Financial Bunker.

Acknowledgements

I would like to thank my wife Kathy for without her patience, understanding and love, this book would not be written. My daughter Tiffany has been at my side helping me with every step along the way. Without my friend Travis Sherman and his continual stream of information on Freedom and the founders, I would not have the perspective I have today. Special thanks to Tim Yurek for the inspiration he provided me with early on, and to Nelson Nash who helped me connect the dots between real Freedom and money.

Finally, I thank my father Terry, who held me accountable to finishing this book. Now I only have one thing to say…

Build Your Bunker.

Rick Bueter

Introduction

In 2007 there was a devastating fire near my home in San Diego. The winds were blowing 60 to 70 miles an hour from the east where the desert resides, to the west where the Pacific Ocean begins.

The fire line was about 1 mile long and over 50 feet tall, with bursts of flames up over 100 feet. It was burning down every house in its path and the firemen could do nothing to stop it. We had taken in some friends whose house was in the path of the fire and they were going to stay with us.

On the night they came over the fire was moving very fast. I could tell that if it kept moving, my house was going to be right in its line. Early the next day we were evacuated. The sky was filled with smoke and our minds were filled with fear. At the moment I received the evacuation notice I went and retrieved our motorhome just down the street and we loaded up. With my kids we had three cars, and the motorhome. We drove out of the neighborhood only to find the one road of escape blocked by thousands of others trying to evacuate.

I knew that if we got stuck there, we could be locked into the traffic with no place to go and the fast moving fire would burn us alive. I could just imagine the panic of thousands of people stuck in cars and traffic with this horrific fire bearing on them. Next to us, I noticed the lane in the opposite direction going TOWARDS the fire had no traffic. It was an empty roadway FREE to use, that nobody was on.

Surely I was not going to start another lane headed away from the fire. However, I was not going to get stuck there waiting for the fire to catch up to us. I did the unthinkable. We made a U turn and headed toward the fire.

Turning a motorhome around on a two-lane road is no simple feat, but there was no other way. We started heading toward the fire and turned down a small side road that immediately set us FREE from it's fury. Nobody else out on that road wanted to THINK differently about getting out when a perfectly good road was sitting right next to them waiting to be used. Fortunately, the fire changed directions and our house and the road were unaffected. That experience taught me a great lesson about Freedom.

We gained our Freedom from the fire because I saw what others did not see. It was the Freedom of an empty road sitting right next to us.

Today the Government is that great wall of fire.

THEY are knocking down the personal Freedom and rights of every American citizen and degrading the statement of Freedom put forth by the Founding Fathers in the Declaration of Independence. The next attack on Freedom will come with the legal confiscation of American's money through taxes. It's already here.

Build Your Bunker.

Section One

It's All About Freedom

Chapter One

Money, Choice, and Freedom

There is a simple formula when it comes to Freedom these days.

The amount of money you have, creates the degree of choice you have in life, which creates the level of Freedom you enjoy.

Money = Choice = Freedom

Whoever controls your money... controls your Freedom. It's that simple.

Who controls your money? Do you? Does your bank? Wall Street? The Government?

For the first four months of the year or longer, we live and work to fill the savings account of the Government until we reach Tax Freedom Day. Until then it can be said our Freedom during that period belongs to the Government. This is true because until you have paid the Government what you owe in taxes, you have no financial Freedom.

The money Government takes from us limits our choices in life. The money we don't have can even affect our health and the quality of food we eat.

How we save money, how we use money, how we consume money, how we lose money, and how it is taxed all determines the degree of Choice we have today and in the future.

Remember that part in the Declaration of Independence about "The Pursuit of Happiness"? Being happy is an element of

Freedom. The amount of fun in life all comes from Freedom and Freedom comes from money.

Money is the key that holds all of this together.

Money is the number one cause of divorce. It's also the number one cause of reduced employee productivity. Lack of money and the resulting stress influences your health, which affects how long you live. In 1910 the top causes of death were pneumonia and influenza. Today they are cancer and heart disease. Both of those are directly correlated to stress. Money is connected to everything, even how long you may live.

Some people say they don't care about money. If that were true, they must not care about people because it's money that frees one from a job to spend time with family and friends. It's money that creates Freedom to pursue causes like the church, a cure for cancer and other causes, which can make the world a better place to live. If you don't care about money, then you really don't care about life and the purpose all of us were placed here for.

In the society we live in today, it's money that creates Freedom. However, the Freedom of every taxpaying American is under attack through their money. We are witnessing a blatant disregard for the Freedom declared and penned by Thomas Jefferson and the Founding Fathers of America.

Life, Liberty and The Pursuit of Happiness

To have real Freedom, the kind of Freedom the Founding Fathers were thinking about you must have **Political Freedom**, **Economic Freedom**, and **Spiritual Freedom**.

Political Freedom

Political Freedom is the Government control over people through laws.

For example, Political Freedom controls movement. When you want to visit another state or another country our political Freedom allows us to do that. You can even choose to live in another state. If you want to buy a gun our political Freedom allows that too; at least for now.

However, in 1913 our congressionally appointed leaders passed the 16th amendment to the Constitution that empowered Government to begin to collect income taxes. It was at that point that the Government began to take away the Freedom Americans enjoyed with money. It also began an accepted process where the Government was empowered to invade American's lives through money. Remember the word "life" from the Declaration? It's interesting that during that same year, The Federal Reserve was created. The year 1913 is a monument in time that marks the shift in controlling the people and their lives through the manipulation of money.

Since then, the Government has been slowly increasing the collection of taxes from Americans. They have been doing it covertly in as many quiet ways as possible. They pass bills in Congress under the guise of "helping you" or making America better. Most recently *The Patient Protection and Affordable Care Act* was passed under President Obama's administration with the intention of providing everyone with healthcare. As you will read, this law could cause the entire economic system of the country to collapse.

If you look back in history, the Government has implemented dozens of failed programs paid for by the confiscation of the human spirit of the American people through taxes. Social

Security, the Energy Program, Federal National Mortgage Association (Fannie Mae), the Post Office, No Child Left Behind, and the War on Poverty, etc. are all programs that are broke or ineffective. These are only a few.

Think of the Personal Freedom that has been sacrificed by Americans at the expense of these wasteful mismanaged programs. In reality, Government officials have wasted the lives of the American people through the continuous leverage of their human spirit. That is the real travesty.

Political Freedom can be summed up as …

1. The degree THEY take money away from YOU (taxes) equals the degree to which you have fewer choices.
2. The degree you have fewer choices equals a lower standard of living.
3. A lower standard of living equals less Freedom.

Today it is quite possible that the average working class American pays over 50% of their income in taxes when you consider all of the different taxes levied on gas, food, clothing, personal property tax, real estate taxes, and utilities. Not only does the Government wastefully spend the tax money they take in, they spend money they don't have by authorizing spending bills financed with money they don't have. Guess who is paying for all of this spending? You, your children and their descendents are going to pay. You are going to pay with your Freedom.

The purpose of understanding how political Freedom works in relation to money is to empower you to think about WHY you do the things you do, with money.

Why do you open 401k and IRA accounts when the cost to use this money (tax rates) is a complete mystery? Why pay cash for something when financing makes more financial sense? Why allow a Wall Street account to continue to skim fees when there is no assurance or guarantee of any future benefit?

Every dollar we lose today determines the level of Freedom we have in the future. It determines the level of choice and the degree of wealth or poverty we live in. Real Freedom is created through Political Freedom.

Economic Freedom

Do you have the full use, control and unrestricted access to your money, at any time? Think about this for a moment.

Do you own an IRA, a 401k or other Government sponsored retirement account? Do you have the full use, control and liquidity of your money? Are you allowed to choose whatever investments you believe are the best in your 401k, or are the investments chosen for you? What about home mortgages? In Australia homebuyers are able to pay off their houses in 1/3 to 1/2 the time because money held in a bank account offsets interest in the loan. Imagine if you were able to have the interest you earn in your 401k offset your mortgage interest. Think of all of the money you could save in interest charged by banks. But THEY don't want Americans to have that option.

Every day Congress is in session, they are looking for ways to stifle the free and unrestricted use of money by writing new laws that control money. Most of these benefit corporate America. Remember, money represents what you create with your life. THEY are trying to confiscate it. THEY want your money locked up so tight that you are forced to let Wall Street skim fees, and forced to borrow from banks.

To win the confiscation game, you must think about ways to make your money work outside of the system THEY have set up. That is how very wealthy people make and keep their money.

Spiritual Freedom

"Fear is the foundation of most Governments."

John Adams

Do the financial markets hold your life in a state of worry or fear? Does the thought of higher taxes concern you? What if social security checks go away, is that a concern? Will you run out of income in retirement? Is your money being taxed for purposes or causes you believe are wrong?

Your money is directly connected to your life, liberty and the pursuit of happiness. If you answered "yes" to any of those questions you are not Spiritually Free. You are held a slave to a higher master who has control over your inner peace. Whether it's the casino of Wall Street, or other financial concerns, a man without Spiritual Peace cannot live in Freedom.

Today banks hold children fresh out of college in financial bondage through Government sponsored education loans. Not surprisingly many of these educational institutions are Wall Street corporations who make millions of dollars selling education financed by Government guaranteed student loans. The money masters have found a way to make slaves out of our children through education. When the mortgage business dried up, Wall Street found a way to create a yield from the lives of our children just like the plantation owner in the days of slavery would have done by putting the children in the field. Hundreds of thousands are now enslaved with decades of debt payments to the Government.

Families across America lured by the dream of easy home ownership into houses they could hardly afford have either been foreclosed on, or live in fear of not being able to make the payments. These financial drug dealers solicit children for credit cards where they become the victims of a system designed to benefit only banks, Wall Street and Government.

The lure of retirement by Wall Street using Government sponsored retirement plans has created an inaccessible pool of savings by the working class that has been skimmed, destroyed and manipulated in the stock market crash. I wrote about this in my book *The Great Wall Street Retirement Scam*. The retirement dreams of millions evaporated in the last decade.

As you will learn in the pages ahead, this has created one of the greatest forms of human bondage in the history of this nation. There is no Spiritual Freedom in any of this.

To live with true Freedom is:

1. **Political Freedom**, to create wealth free from Government taxes
2. **Economic Freedom,** to have the use, control and liquidity of money and live the life we have chosen to create
3. **Spiritual Freedom**, a life filled with possibilities, hope, imagination and empowerment free from the fear and worry created by banks, Wall Street and Government.

Money = Choice = Freedom

Now think about what you have just learned.

If Thomas Jefferson were here today, these are the questions he would be asking…

Is your money politically free? Is it free from taxes?
Is your money economically free? Do you have the use, control and liquidity of all your money?

Is your money spiritually free? Does your money fill you with feelings of confidence and peace?

You will find all of this inside a Financial Bunker.

Build Your Bunker.

Chapter Two

The Great Confiscation Period Is Here!

"I would argue that the most serious threat to the United States is not someone hiding in a cave in Afghanistan, or Pakistan, but our own fiscal responsibility." –

David Walker, Former Comptroller of the Currency and
Head of the Government Accountability Office 1998 - 2008

...May 2010, Greece agrees to a bailout from the European Union and International Monetary Fund after agreeing to an austerity program to solve its overspending problems. The sale of Government assets, higher taxes and reduced spending ensued. The time element demanded in the bailout was too short and a second bailout occurred in February 2012. Today the people of Greece are suffering with reduced Government services, lower standards of living and higher taxes on those who have money.

...In 2013, Cyprus, a small island country in the middle of the Mediterranean Sea experienced a banking crisis which forced the Government to either collapse it's banking system or confiscate money from the bank accounts of the wealthy. They chose to confiscate money from those who could afford to lose money, the wealthier minority.

The direct confiscation of wealth from citizens whose Government participates in the Euro zone should be taken as a sign. A precedent for future countries to consider, but also a sign there are no more bailouts.

The United States of America is not Cyprus, nor is it Greece, but financially the debt of America is approaching nearly the same as a percentage of our gross domestic product, the measure of the output of goods and services. **This is the problem.**

According to an International Monetary Fund report issued September 2011[1], within 10 years the U.S. is on track to hit the debt to GDP levels that Greece did before it's debt crisis; but when you add in the debt owed to Social Security, Medicare and other federal trust funds, the U.S. is within three years of reaching the debt-to-GDP level of Greece at the time of its crisis.

By 2022, the Government of The United States of America will no longer be able to pay it's bills.

In 10 years social security will be paying out more than it is taking in. This cost will be adding to the annual federal deficit. Medicare and Medicaid will only make things worse. Our children will live in a country where they have a Government they cannot afford. The thought of a college education will become a distant wish. Owning a home will become rare, and the quality of life will be substantially reduced because of the high costs created by highly inflated dollars.

Just how bad is it?

The way economists look at this problem is by taking a measurement of the gross domestic product (GDP). Most would agree that maintaining public debt at around 60% of GDP is manageable and acceptable. At the time of this writing, the U.S. debt-to-GDP is 103%. By 2016 with Medicare and Social Security and other federally mandated programs, the debt-to-GDP will be nearing 150%, the level that put Greece over the edge.

What does this mean to every American?

---

1 IMF September 2011 World Economic Outlook Slowing Growth, Rising Risks

For the 2012 fiscal year, the Government would need to have collected $3,500 from every man, woman and child today, in order to pay for their overspending. That amount is in addition to the taxes already collected.

To pay off the entire Government debt today, they would need to collect $51,100 from every man, woman and child.

To pay for the unfunded future liabilities that exist in Government programs including Social Security, Medicare and Medicaid, the Government would need to collect $222,000 from every man, woman and child[2].

How Did We Get Here?

Amazingly, the Government had annual surpluses in the late 90's and into early 2000. These surpluses were the result of the Budget Enforcement Act of 1990. In the 1990's congress enacted what is called PAYGO (pay-as-you-go). It is a rule that governs mandatory spending and tax legislation. This rule would require that all increases in direct spending or revenue decreases to be offset by other spending decreases or revenue increases. This rule worked and held congressional spending in check. However, it expired in 2002 and the rule was not reestablished until 2007, but with much less control than was in place previously.

In 2000, George W. Bush was elected President. At that time the federal deficit was 5.6 trillion dollars. To win support, Bush pushed the largest tax cut in decades known as "The Bush Tax Cuts". Right after that in 2001, the United States waged an undeclared war against Iraq and Afghanistan that cost hundreds of billions in unbudgeted expenditures. By 2003, Bush had passed 3 major tax cuts.

2 The Department of Treasury, 2012, Financial Report of the United States Government

By May of 2003, the federal debt was 6.5 trillion dollars. During this short period the Federal Reserve cut interest rates 21 times. The result was a steep decline in America's currency, and the unseen formation of a real estate "bubble".

As time went on, Bush's popularity was falling as a result of the war. To gain more support, Bush signed the most expensive social program of its time, Medicare Part D, the prescription drug program. Bush was re-elected November 4th, 2004.

By 2007, the federal deficit had grown to 8.7 trillion.

During Bush's reign as President, the federal debt increased from 5.6 to 8.7 trillion, a stunning 55 percent increase. As of 2013, the federal debt has grown to over 16 trillion dollars. This is a 185 percent increase.

To give you an example of how this has gotten out of control, take a look at the U.S. Debt Level chart in Figure 1.

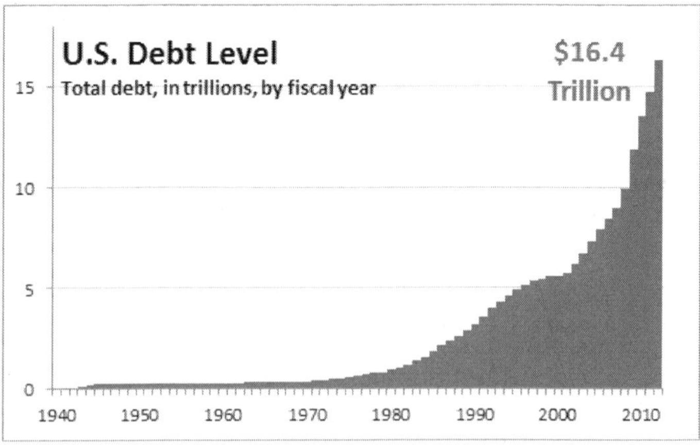

Figure 1

The Coming Financial Crisis

The U.S. Federal Spending- Fiscal Year 2012 chart in Figure 2 shows the amount of Government spending by category for just 2012. The major categories of concern are Medicare, Medicaid, Social Security, Defense, and interest costs. These are the categories that represent the highest future risks, and costs to the federal debt.

Today, the Government debt is being financed by very low, crisis level interest rates. As of this writing, the 10 year treasury bond is 2.50%, and the one year treasury bill pays a mere 14 basis points. That's 14 cents on a $100 savings deposit.

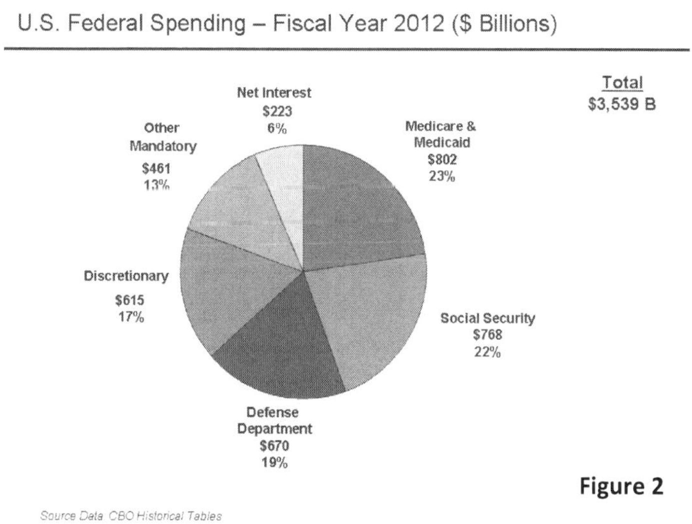

Figure 2

When interest rates finally do go up, the interest cost to the Government will also go up. The rising interest costs mean more Government spending on something that produces nothing. Think about your own mortgage if you have one. When you pay mortgage interest, what do you get in return? You make your Banker richer. That is exactly what we will be doing with those who hold the debt of America.

Each day there are 10,000 baby boomers entering into their retirement years and becoming eligible for federal Medicare and Medicaid benefits. The chart above only shows what the spending is for 2012, not the next 17 years when the baby boomers will be flooding the system with health care needs. Social Security expenditures will continue to go up as well. The unfunded liabilities for Social Security and Medicare Part A, B and D are estimated at 85.7 trillion dollars[3].

Political Ramifications Of America's Debt

Historical precedence of using debt as a weapon of influence against other countries exists. The country that used such a weapon was the United States of America.

In 1956 allies of the U.S., the United Kingdom and France were in dispute over the Suez Canal with Egypt. Russia took the side in support of Egypt. The timing of this event was happening as a nuclear arms race was under way between Russia and the U.S. Further tensions between U.S. allies and Russia could have started a nuclear war.

The U.S. requested that the U.K. and France stand down over their dispute. The allies chose to stand firm. During this period the U.S. was a major investor in the pound, the currency of the U.K. Upon the U.S. threatening to sell off its holdings of the pound by dumping them into the financial markets, the allies backed down from their dispute. If the U.S. had followed through, it would have crushed the economy of the U.K from the resulting devaluation of their currency.

3 Department of Treasury Financial Report of the United States Government. Medicare numbers based on the Office of the Chief Actuary's alternative cost estimate in Medicare Trustees' Report

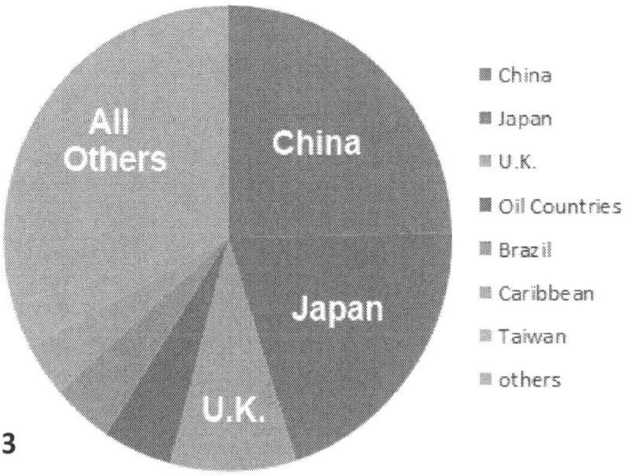

Figure 3

Figure 3 shows a chart of the top holders of U.S. debt. As you can see, China which is a communist country, is the single largest holder of U.S debt. Suffice it to say, we should always seek good relations with our creditors.

Financial Ratings

Another factor to consider is the financial rating of America. On August 5th, 2011 Standard & Poor's, the independent private company that issues financial ratings on corporations and Governments, downgraded the U.S. Federal Government from a AAA (outstanding) rating to a AA+ (excellent). This downgrade occurred four days after congress voted to increase the debt ceiling. As mentioned earlier, this increase in debt moved the U.S. away from a debt-to-GDP ratio that was favorable, to one that increased the risk of default. While congress was debating the issue, the stock market experienced substantial volatility where at one point the Dow Jones Averages had declined 700 points.

The result of a downgrade in financial ratings means that taxpayers, the owners of this debt and the ones responsible for paying bondholders back, will have to pay higher interest to others to buy our bonds. The money will come from taxes. It will be the legal confiscation of money from you and I to pay for something that creates no economic potential. It is the same as the interest you pay to banks for a mortgage. The money does nothing to your personal balance sheet.

This is even worse for the country. As more taxes are squeezed out of American's pockets, it makes the people of this country weaker. New ideas, entrepreneurship, business owners, independence, the very foundation of principles of the Founding Fathers melt away even faster. The rating agencies will look at this additional taxation and conclude as they already have by the first rating decline, that America is becoming weaker financially. This issue becomes a vicious cycle.

Where Will The Money Come From?

Hopefully you have an insight as to the gravity of where our country lies financially. The question becomes, how do we get out of this mess?

Some believe the problem is one of leadership. It was President Bush who allowed the spending to get out of hand. Will President Obama be any different? Do he and his predecessor have what it takes to make the politically unattractive decisions that will cut spending on programs promised to Americans? What would be the civilian response to decreased Government services? Riots, civil unrest, domestic terrorism? The answer probably lies with what happened in Greece, Spain and Cyprus.

On the other hand, should the Government raise taxes? Should they take money out of the hands of the wage earners to pay for the gargantuan financial commitment of unfunded Medicare and other social programs?

Take a look at the chart of historical income tax rates in Figure 4. As you can see, relative to the actual rate that taxes are paid at, we live in one of the lowest periods of income taxes in a generation.

However, over the last few decades the Government has been slowly taking away deductions such as auto loan interest. They've created the alternative minimum tax and placed a ceiling on home mortgage interest deductions. These are just a few of the tax laws that have been slowly worked in to take more money away from Americans.

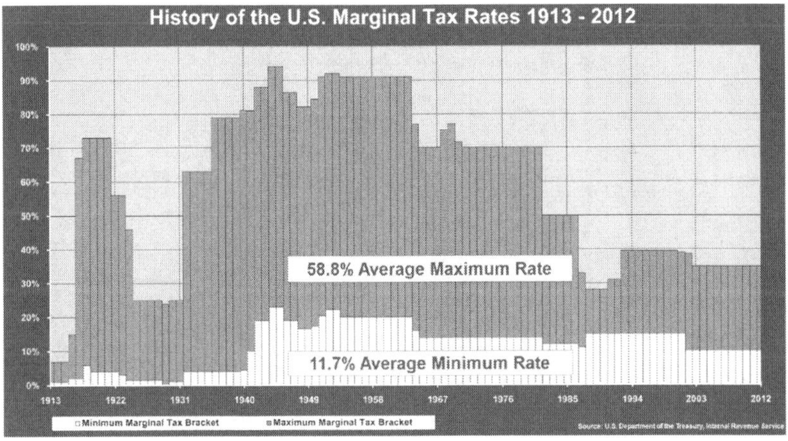

Figure 4

Logic dictates that taxes must go up.

Payroll taxes, income taxes, estate taxes, value added taxes, and excise taxes are the weapons of mass personal financial destruction that the Government has at its disposal. "Make no mistake", the Government can and will take your money. History proves it. In 1933, the Government confiscated gold from Americans under the guise of wartime needs. Americans who owned gold were angry and many of them were immigrants who came to America to build a future.

Some of those who were new to America understood how Governments could inflate the money supply as this had been done in Germany after World War I. These new Americans put some of their money into gold only to be disappointed by a Government that promised Life, Liberty and The Pursuit of Happiness.

There should be no misunderstanding. This **IS** within the power of our Government.

POSTMASTER: PLEASE POST IN A CONSPICUOUS PLACE—JAMES A. FARLEY, Postmaster General

UNDER EXECUTIVE ORDER OF THE PRESIDENT

Issued April 5, 1933

all persons are required to deliver

ON OR BEFORE MAY 1, 1933

all GOLD COIN, GOLD BULLION, AND GOLD CERTIFICATES now owned by them to a Federal Reserve Bank, branch or agency, or to any member bank of the Federal Reserve System.

Executive Order

FRANKLIN D. ROOSEVELT

For Further Information Consult Your Local Bank

GOLD CERTIFICATES may be identified by the words "GOLD CERTIFICATE" appearing thereon. The serial number and the Treasury seal on the face of a GOLD CERTIFICATE are printed in YELLOW. Be careful not to confuse GOLD CERTIFICATES with other issues which are redeemable in gold but which are not GOLD CERTIFICATES. Federal Reserve Notes and United States Notes are "redeemable in gold" but are not "GOLD CERTIFICATES" and are not required to be surrendered

Special attention is directed to the exceptions allowed under Section 2 of the Executive Order

CRIMINAL PENALTIES FOR VIOLATION OF EXECUTIVE ORDER $10,000 fine or 10 years imprisonment, or both, as provided in Section 9 of the order

Secretary of the Treasury.

U.S. Government Printing Office: 1933 2-16064

Figure 5

The taxing power of Congress IS the legal confiscation of money.

A Financial Bunker will be one of the last places the Government will come for money. Billions of dollars sit within Financial Bunkers held by the wealthiest Americans and financial institutions. As you will come to know, it is one of the last protected Freedoms found in the tax code of the United States of America.

Build Your Bunker.

Chapter Three

The Future Cost Of Healthcare

On March 23, 2010 President Obama signed into law the Patient Protection and Affordable Care Act (PPACA). This act started a tectonic change in the healthcare system of America. It is the most significant Government expansion and overhaul of the healthcare system since the passage of Medicare and Medicaid in 1965.

The purpose of the PPACA is to provide healthcare and coverage for all Americans. It is complicated, it is vague, and the basic document is 2,700 pages long. The implementation of the act will require layers of Government bureaucracies to manage the program. In the midst of not even having a plan to pay for existing social programs, the Government has added what is arguably the most complex social program in the history of America.

What this program will look like when it is fully operational is unclear. What is clear is that the demand for medical services will increase. Without the addition of credentialed medical professionals, a first year economist would tell you that the level of service must decrease. What this means to Americans and the future of the healthcare system is a reduction in choice.

When there is only one specialist and 100 sick patients, the only choice is to wait in line. If you speak to someone from Canada where the Government controls the healthcare system, they will tell you that it can take months to get medical services such as a hip or knee replacement. For the baby boomers of America used to quick access to medicine, that is a tectonic loss of Freedom.

Quality Of Healthcare

Another problem is that many seasoned, fully credentialed doctors are leaving the business of medicine. They are being driven out by the underpayments of Medicare, the bureaucracy of Government, and the uncontrolled cost of medical liability insurance. Of course with a Government operated healthcare facility, you probably won't be able to successfully file a malpractice lawsuit. But without that legal process to hold medicine accountable, you end up with a medical system where the level of attention to good medical care becomes unimportant.

The cost of the Government program is another factor.

The independent office of the chief actuary of Medicare headed by Richard Foster has said the PPACA will cost trillions more than claimed[4]. Time will tell and so will your taxes. Interestingly, Foster who acted as chief actuary resigned in January 2013 after 18 years of service. During his tenure he fought political battles with President George W. Bush over the true costs of Medicare part D.

One new tax that is part of the PPACA will begin in 2014; it is a 3.8% surtax on certain investment income. This affects married couples earning over $250,000 and singles earning over $200,000. This tax is just for starters. Since the full cost of the program is yet to be determined, one should expect additional forms of taxes in the future.

The Wagon Trail Of Retirees

As the 10,000 baby boomers head into retirement the demands on the system will become clear. People will be seeing fewer doctors and more physician's assistants. Serious illnesses might

4 David Walker Former U.S. Comptroller General Come Back America Initiative 2012

be overlooked resulting in higher healthcare costs. Specialists will be in high demand and waiting periods will increase. One should also expect more scrutiny over services, much the same way HMO referral systems operate today but with more bureaucracy. More importantly, because Government will oversee the system, the accountability for the practice of high quality medical attention should be expected to decline. This is not unlike most Government services.

Health Care Choice - The Government's Plan or Your Own?

Today 75% of the money spent on medicine in America goes toward the treatment of chronic diseases. That is heart attack, cancer, stroke, diabetes and arthritis. 7 out of 10 who develop these diseases die from them. This is right down the gutter of the baby boomers. Will the system be able to absorb this? Will you have choice in treatment and wellness services, or will it be the Government's plan? What if there is an experimental treatment for a cancer cure? Will the Government's plan pay for it? Interestingly, 62 percent of bankruptcies are from Medical events[5]. If you have unlimited assets then you probably will have choice, but if not, then what?

If you have a family, this is not just about you, it's about your children and grandchildren as well. If you care about their future, the best advice is to think independently. Learn the limitations of the programs. Expect to get "Government like" service from the system and prepare for catastrophic events. There are medical events that will occur with this new thinking about healthcare that no one has even thought about. Only then will the true nature of the program be unveiled.

---

5 Medical Bankruptcy in the US 2007, The American Journal of Medicine 2009

The IRS

The Internal Revenue Service will play a large part in the policing of the healthcare system. There will be new forms to be filed with your tax return. There will be more explanation required for treatments and drugs. Right now doctors know the Government is looking over their shoulder scrutinizing every test and treatment.

Each new day doctors are held more accountable financially to the cost of treatment. Will it be the doctor who decides if you should get a major surgery that can save your life, or will it be the IRS who has a table they refer to that tells them if it is actuarially sound to perform the treatment based on your age and current health condition?

More and more information is required to be divulged to the IRS since they are responsible for the correct payment by employers and individuals upon the implementation of the healthcare system in 2014. As we move forward in time, the involvement of the IRS in one's personal health will become clearer to Americans as more Government officials control the revenues of this new Government idea.

In the Declaration of Independence the words "Life, Liberty, and the Pursuit of Happiness" appear. It's painfully apparent that Liberty is under attack through money. Now "Life" is also being taken over by Government as well. A properly structured bunker can create more choices when it comes to certain healthcare issues. Take note of this and most importantly, take action.

Build Your Bunker.

Chapter Four

When The Bubble Pops

For those not acquainted with what the Federal Reserve *is* or *does*, here is an elementary review...

The Federal Reserve is neither a bank where American citizens make deposits and loans, nor a branch of Government. It is an independent entity empowered and created by Congress in 1913 to control the supply of money in America. It is held accountable to the people of America through the oversight powers of Congress. Through the activities of The Federal Reserve, money is controlled and moved through 12 regional Federal Reserve Banks who then serve the retail banks of America supplying them with money for loans. The purpose of its existence according to their charter is to promote maximum employment, stable prices and moderate long-term interest rates.

The free reign of The Federal Reserve's actions within the banking system has allowed the greatest financial bubbles to occur in history. Of recent history, the 1929 stock market crash, and the financial bubble America is floating on today. In their power, is the ability to control the flow of money into the economy of America and the world. The Federal Reserve manipulates interest rates when the economy heats up, and it decreases interest rates when the economy slows. It has three basic methods of operation in which to maintain this manipulation.

The first is the discount rate. This is the rate charged by the Federal Reserve when it makes loans to commercial banks. The second is the Fed Funds rate, which is the rate charged between banks. The third method and the most controversial today, is open market operations. The Federal Open Market Committee manipulates interest rates through the purchase and sale of securities in the financial markets.

There are several good books to read about the Federal Reserve that go into great detail. Ron Paul, the former presidential candidate and Texas congressional representative wrote "End The Fed". Another great book is "The Creature From Jekyll Island" by G. Edward Griffin.

For our purposes a basic understanding of what the Federal Reserve does today is what is important.

Fractional Reserve Banking

Let's say you make a deposit in The Bank Of XYZ. Did you know that the bank could loan that dollar out 9 times? So the question becomes, if they only have 1 dollar, how can they loan out 9 dollars? You are about to learn why banking is the most profitable, lowest risk business on the planet.

The Bank of XYZ needed 9 dollars, so they went and borrowed it from The Federal Reserve. At the time of the printing of this book, The "Fed" charges The Bank of XYZ just .75%. The Bank of XYZ then lends that money out at 4-6%. If you do the math, this is an 800% return on the investment cost. Remember the no risk part...the bank didn't even use their own money. They simply borrowed from the "Fed". That is why banking is so lucrative. This process is called "fractional reserve banking".

But where does "The Fed" get their money?

The answer...They print it from thin air.

It's true and what that ultimately means is that the value of every dollar you earn today, is being diluted by the congressionally appointed "Fed" because only <u>*they*</u> have the power to print money from nothing.

Your human spirit, your blood sweat and tears, your ability to create your own Freedom through money is being stolen and diluted through this process.

Now let's get to the stuff that will make your eyes pop wide open.

The Next Giant Bubble

Since the near collapse of the banking system, and the stock market crash in 2009, the "Fed" has been involved in a historic open market program to control interest rates. Not only have fed funds rates and the discount rate been held at historically low levels, the "Fed" has implemented "quantitative easing" otherwise known as "QE" programs.

The first QE program (QE1)was launched November 25, 2008. During this period the "Fed" purchased 1.24 trillion dollars of mortgage-backed securities and $175 billion of agency (Fannie Mae and Freddie Mac Government guaranteed mortgage loans). The goal was to take the paper off the books of banks to make them solvent and to hold interest rates low. That program ended March 31st, 2010.

After further evaluation, the "Fed" began another QE program. On November 3rd, 2010 QE2 was implemented and the Fed began an open market purchase program of $600 billion dollars of long-term Treasury securities. The Fed said that QE2 would help promote a stronger pace of economic recovery. Mortgage rates spiked more than half a percentage point in a little over a month after the implementation of QE2. By the end of the program (June 30, 2011), mortgage rates had tumbled and reached record lows.

On September 13, 2012 the "Fed" launched another round of open market purchases QE3, to keep rates down hoping that new cash injections into the system would give the economy a boost. At the time this book was written, the program had not yet ended. The "Fed" is intending to buy billions more in mortgage-backed investments until the economy shows improvement. That is *on top of* the billions it has already been buying.

By the way...where does the "Fed" get money from again?

Here Is The Problem...

Someday the "Fed" must unwind all this money and move it back into the market. That means THEY must sell the bonds and investments they have purchased. What will that mean?

In the short term, the Fed cannot sell what they have purchased. They must be buyers of bonds to make the banks healthy and to do that, the banks must be making loans, lots of loans. Right now the amount of loans being made is not accelerating with any great volume.

What about 5 to 10 years from now? What about 10-20 years from now?

Take a look at the chart in Figure 6. This illustrates the massive influx of money into the financial system by the Fed beginning with the QE programs. Over 2 trillion dollars has entered the system from the Fed's programs. This is money, printed from thin air, used to buy bonds to artificially lower interest rates, and someday they will have to sell these bonds. It is unparalleled in the history of America.

Today, the Fed is backfilling all of the losses in the banking system through their manipulation of interest rates charged to banks at almost zero. This near free cost of money being made available to the commercial banks is being used by banks to create a profitable arbitrage between what they can borrow from the Fed, and what they can earn by investing money into the bond markets. What is ironic is that home loans are harder to come by than ever before.

The Fed has created a massive bubble of money in the system. Through the ease of money via the Fed, another stock market bubble is forming. As of this printing, the Standard & Poor's index has risen over 130% from the bottom of the stock market crash. We have now entered into a financial world of bubbles and crashes. At some point, there will have to be a reconciliation of all of this.

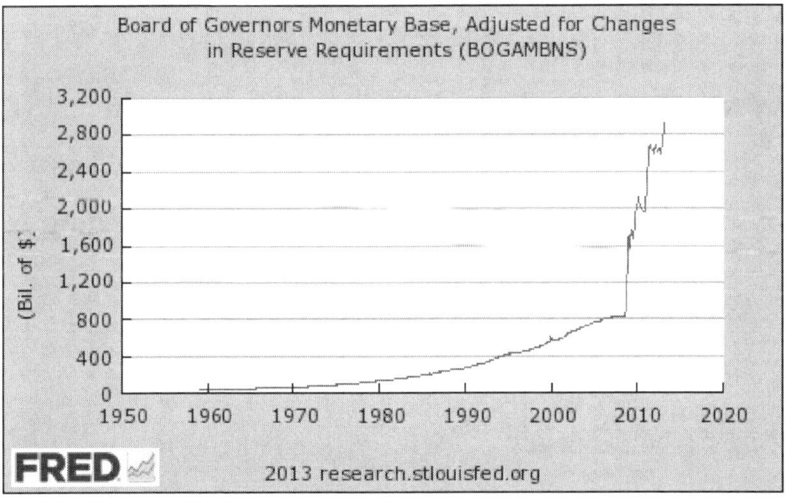

Figure 6

A Warning To Bond Investors

The result of this manipulation has created a massive bubble, this time in bonds. Over the long term, individuals who invest in bonds are in serious trouble. To begin with, most individuals cannot diversify and ladder enough to weather the coming bond correction. With interest rates pushed to near zero percent, bond investors who bought bonds at par will see substantial decreases when rates start to rise. Even with a laddered bond portfolio, the market losses could be substantial. If your time horizon is 100 years like that of a life insurance company, or pension plan you will be ok.

One day there will come a point...

where there is no more arbitrage for bankers to profit from,

where everyone who owns bonds, will want to sell them,

where business owners won't be able to get credit,

when the stock market tumbles,

when the bond market will crash,

when Americans will experience a historic rise in interest rates,

when everything about life, money and Freedom will change,

when those who have prepared will discover opportunity.

Build Your Bunker.

Chapter Five

The American Retirement Crisis

"The Government has every person in America locking up money for retirement in IRA and 401k plans, where the rate of tax is yet to be determined"

Rick Bueter

Current State Of Retirement

From the time you start working until the day you retire, every financial planner in America will tell you to put money in a Government sponsored retirement account. These are known as 401k/IRA/TSA and other plans. In my book *The Great Wall Street Retirement Scam,* I explain why Wall Street programs could never achieve the retirement objectives they were propagandized to deliver.

Since the publication of *The Great Wall Street Retirement Scam*, the media is finally beginning to question America's retirement system. More books have now been published which question the principles promoted by nearly every financial professional. Recently, The Public Broadcasting System recently aired a scathing documentary into Wall Street and retirement planning on its television program "Frontline".

After having had years to think about money, Government, Wall Street and retirement, it appears that a conspiracy is going on.

From the day you start working until the day you retire, we are told by every financial planner in America to save for retirement in IRAs and 401k plans. Let's examine that thinking for a moment. Not withstanding that the idea of retirement comes from socialist thinking, let's say you follow that advice.

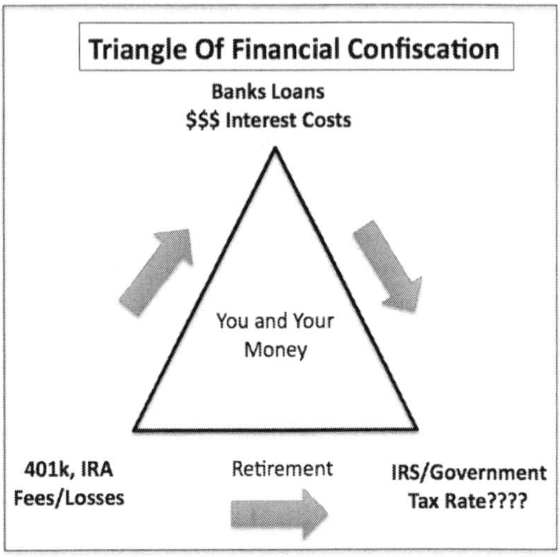

Figure 7

So for the next 40 years you save money in the Government sponsored retirement plans. During this time, your money is largely inaccessible. You have given up its use, control and liquidity as you can see in the bottom left corner of what we call "The Triangle of Confiscation" in Figure 7. You will begin to understand the title in a moment.

The bottom left hand corner of the triangle is where nearly 90 percent of the savings resides for working Americans with 401k-type retirement accounts. This means, outside of these plans they only have 10 percent of their money freely accessible. This illiquidity is making the banks rich.

About 401k Fees

When it comes to fees in retirement savings plans Congressional Representative George Miller of California says, "You may have losses on these plans, but you will certainly have fees." Just recently laws were implemented to require the full disclosure of these fees, and an average couple's estimated lifetime fees could be over $150,000[6]. This could represent years of income for some people. Think of the Freedom that is being lost through that money.

Now move to the top of the triangle, to the banks.

During life you may have a need to make a major purchase such as a car, or a home. Because you were encouraged to save money in illiquid retirement plans through the lure of a tax deduction, you must now go to banks and pay them interest to use a stranger's money. Quite possibly the money the bank loans you is your own money which is locked up in the Government sponsored IRA or 401k plan.

Because you have no access to your money in IRAs, and to a great extent other Government sponsored retirement plans, banks benefit through interest charged so you can finance the major purchases in life. Keep in mind, you might have a significant amount of money in a retirement plan, but you can't use it. Because of this lack of Freedom with their own money, over a lifetime average Americans will give up over $500,000[7] in bank interest charges to use the money of strangers, instead of using their own.

Government Wins In The End

Today, many of those who are retired and have saved money in this system are making the Government richer over the taxes they are now forced to pay on distributions they don't need.

Whatever resides in these plans after death, will then be dumped on the next generation who is completely unprepared to properly

6 Demos.org, a research organization.

7 Based on refinance or move every 7 years, two car household financing 22 cars over a lifetime. Excludes, college, credit card and other consumer interest costs.

inherit this money. That generation will be boiled in the kettle by taxes on these retirement accounts. That too is all about education. This is an unfortunate loss of one's lifetime legacy of human effort. It is a feast for the Government.

Think about the minutes, hours, days, months, and years of Financial Freedom that is being vaporized in this system. The fees on 401ks, the interest charged by banks because you cannot use your own money, and the harvest of taxes on your savings all add up to lost Freedom. Freedom that is being vaporized by a Government sponsored plan.

Of course the idea used to promote these plans was that taxes would be lower in retirement, right?

But wait…there's more. Think about this question for a moment.

Would you ever buy a car, sign a contract and drive it off the lot, WITHOUT knowing the purchase price?

How about buying a house?

Would you ever buy a house, sign a contract and move in without knowing the exact purchase price to the penny? If you are reading this book you might think of yourself as a good steward of your money.

Now look at the bottom right corner of the triangle. That is the Government.

The Government has every person in America locking up money for retirement in IRA and 401k plans, where the rate of tax is *yet* to be determined.

You are buying something where you have no idea what it will cost you. And... it's your money.

Roth IRA? Think Again

Some people think they have the answer with the "Roth" plan because it is tax-free.

Who do you think writes the rules for these plans? The Government does. Who decides when to change the rules? The Government. The rules change to meet the needs of the Government.

What are the Government's needs today?

More money!

Unless you are older and receiving social security, you wouldn't know social security was promised as a tax-free benefit. When President Roosevelt signed the social security bill in 1935, the claim was that there wouldn't be any taxes on social security benefits, ever. Today, you pay taxes on social security when you pay into the system. When you receive social security, (and you are not in poverty) you pay taxes on that money again. Double taxation at its finest.

President Reagan started this change in taxes on social security when up to 50% of it could be taxed based on a "means" formula. Meaning if you have money, you pay taxes on it. What is ironic about this is that the promises made by the political leaders who implemented the system are known only to those who are now deceased, or near the end of their lives. These octogenarians are too few in number to make trouble for political leaders. This is the potential problem with the "Roth IRA". Congress could change the tax laws just like they changed social security.

The Triangle Of Confiscation illustrates an economic system of money designed to attract, manipulate and control the wealth of Americans all for the benefit of the masters. It is a system for dependents that will pay dearly with their lives as the Government prints infinite amounts of money. It's a system where American's lives are siphoned through money by banks, Wall Street and Government with nothing to show for it.

Now apply what you have learned about Freedom to the triangle in Figure 7. Do you see the triangle exuding Political, Economic and Spiritual Freedom? Does the triangle advocate Life, Liberty and the Pursuit of Freedom? Or is it doing exactly the opposite while making Wall Street, Banks and the Government richer?

Is There Freedom If…

- The Government can change the rules to suit their needs?
- You do not have choice nor the ability to invest your money into ideas that might create more Freedom for YOU?
- You cannot get your money when you need it?
- If the investments within the system cause worry or fear?
- You can't make your mortgage or car payment, and your <u>own</u> money is inaccessible to you?

So the question is,
Do you want to save for Retirement, or save for Freedom?

It is quite possible Freedom could occur long before you even think about retirement.

Time is of the essence. Half of all workers have less than $10,000 saved for retirement. Of those 55 or older, 60 percent have less than $100,000 saved. This will put a huge demand on social services as those who have no money, will grow old living the final years of life looking for Government assistance and housing. **It doesn't take much to imagine where the Government will find the money to pay for those who did not save.**

The money will come from those who have money, not those who don't. Act now. Make your money as hard as possible for the government to take. A Financial Bunker holds immense Freedom to use, control and access your money all without income taxes.

Build Your Bunker.

Section Two

Financial Principles

Chapter Six

Listen To Albert

The most powerful force in the universe is compound interest.

Albert Einstein

$$M = P(1 + i)^n$$

In this section you will learn the principles of money, compounding and banking which will prepare you for a complete understanding of one of the most powerful elements found in Financial Bunker building.

To understand the economic potential and use of a personal Financial Bunker, we must first understand some basic principles of money. These are well understood by the money masters and are used to create an immense amount of wealth for themselves. Once these principles are mastered, you will be able to fully appreciate the information in the upcoming chapters.

When scientists try to define principles of the universe they use numbers.

An example of this comes from geometry and is called the Pythagorean theorem, $a^2+b^2=c^2$. Using this formula, you can determine the length of the long side of a triangle. It does this perfectly every single time without failure into eternity. It is predictable, it is certain, and it is proven. No matter what the number is for a^2 and b^2, you always get the same correct result for c^2.

When it comes to money, we think of earning interest. Compound interest comes from math. It is based on a certain formula just like the Pythagorean theorem.

This is the formula: $M = P(1 + i)^n$

Do you see the words, potential, opportunity, or possibilities in this formula? They don't exist.

Compound interest is perfect. It does not, nor can it, hold any thinking contrived by man to alter its mathematical outcome. That is why it's so powerful!

Now you are about to learn one of the most valuable lessons about money and wealth building you have ever seen.

The Compounded Penny Illustration

Let's say you took a penny and doubled it every day for the next 30 days. How much money would you have at the end of that period?

So you start out on day one with 1 penny.

By day five you have 16 cents,
By day 10 you have $5.12,
By day 15 you have $163.84,
By day 20 you have $5,242.88,
By day 22 you have $20,971.52.

But now you have to stop.

Yes the goal was to get to day thirty, but you find out you have to buy a new car. So you must take the $20,971.52 to the car dealer and you no longer can continue compounding your money. Now you have to start again with one penny.

You have stopped the compounding of your money. Your human interaction caused the most powerful force in the universe to crumble!

Please don't take this personally; because once you understand the principles of compounding, you would probably have given both your right and left arms to prevent anything from affecting the math of compounding.

Had you been able to allow the penny to continue to compound until day 30, you would have had $10,738,418!

Einstein clearly understood this as exemplified by his quote:

"The most powerful force in the universe is compound interest."

The lesson here is that in order to realize this force, you must NEVER reset the compounding of your money. It must be allowed to grow and compound just like the penny until the end of your life.

If there is any doubt in your mind about the effect of Political Freedom (aka taxes) on your money, just take a look at the numbers below. Doubling the penny with taxes produces a wealth loss of $10,622,045.

30 Days With Tax Freedom	**$10,738,418**
30 Days Without Tax Freedom	**$116,373**[8]

8 28 percent tax bracket

Another aspect of compounding is that over the short-term, it appears that the numbers are not that impressive. By day 10 you had just $5.12 and were one-third through the 30 days. This is when most people lose interest (no pun intended); they see the glitter or allure of somewhere else to put money. They take their money out and stop the compounding cycle. They give up.

In the example above we used taxes to illustrate how compounding becomes affected and its power is diminished. For those who think Wall Street is the answer, imagine now adding fees on top of the taxes to the compounding formula. This kills the power of compounding.

If people just stopped resetting the compounding they would be so much wealthier.

Compounding makes you rich when you need to be rich, when you are old. But remember, you cannot compound a Wall Street investment because it is not perfect math. The stock market crash of 2009 illustrates this, as these investments are subject to gains and losses. To try and impute any percentage return from these into the future is just fraud. It can't be done using compound interest.

Now apply what you have just learned about Freedom to compounding.

Is compounding Spiritually Free? This is true as long as humans do not get involved.

Is it Economically Free? Yes. When left to do its job it creates infinite wealth into eternity.

Is it Politically Free? The answer depends where the money is compounding and if it is taxed. If it is taxed, the answer is no. However if you apply compounding to an economic system such as the Financial Bunker, then the answer is yes. Compounding used within that context makes it Politically Free.

The power of compounding when uninterrupted by human behavior and allowed to run over long periods of time creates numbers that are unimaginable. They are unimaginable because people don't understand all the uses and applications of compounding with money. Even financial professionals don't understand why compounding is so powerful. Again, the power comes from whether or not you have a system that can allow money to compound over a lifetime without resetting and starting over again.

This is one of the most powerful elements you will find in a Financial Bunker. It is the key to creating massive sums of wealth untouchable by income taxes. And, you can still have the use of your money, WITHOUT resetting the compounding!

Build Your Bunker.

Chapter Seven

A Valuable Lesson In Banking and Loans

To appreciate the financial aspects of a personal Financial Bunker, a lesson in banking and loans is necessary.

For purposes of this section, you must recognize that the banking and finance world we live in today is not normal. Never in most people's lifetime have there been interest rates and financing at such low levels. The examples here are merely to illustrate the concepts as they would play out in a more normal interest rate environment. Building a Bunker, is about preparing for the future in all aspects of personal finance.

Give Up or Pay Up

Every major purchase in life is financed whether you pay cash, or take out a loan.

Whether it's cars, homes, college educations, business purchases, everything we pay money for is financed. Here is why...

If you pay cash, you *give up* the interest you could have been earning on that money.

If you finance, you *pay interest* on a loan.

You either **give up**, or **pay up** interest. This is a very important concept.

Quite frequently we hear the gurus say it's better to pay cash and get out of debt. Let's examine that philosophy.

Let's say you want to buy a $30,000 car.

You go to your bank to withdraw $30,000 from your savings earning 4%, in order to pay cash for a new car.

Your banker says you would be better off to leave your money in your savings account and take out a loan at 6%. He says you will have more money at the end of the loan period than you would by paying cash.

Do you believe him?

When you first hear this, you probably think the banker just wants to sell you a loan right? Take a look at the math below.

If you take out a $30,000 loan at 6% and repay it over 60 months the total repayments to the bank are $34,799. The interest cost was $4,799. That is $4,799 that you no longer have in your wallet.

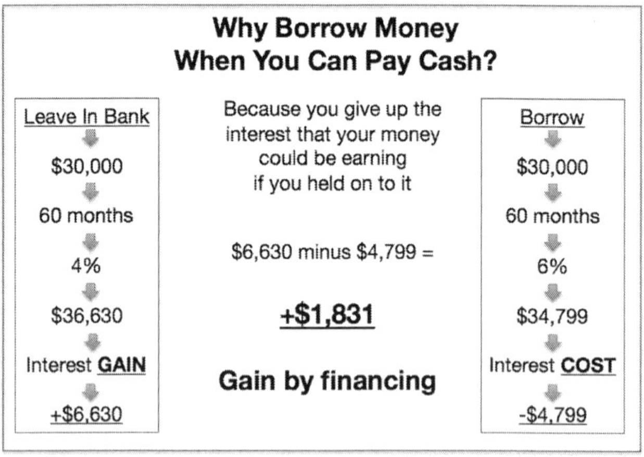

Figure 8

If you leave your $30,000 sitting in the bank over the next 60 months earning just 4%, you will have $36,630. That is $6,630 added to your wallet.

Now, take the $6,630 you gained by leaving your money in the bank, and subtract the $4,799 cost to finance the car and what do you have? A profit of $1,831. You now have $1,831 more than you would have, if you paid cash for the car.

Now consider the following...

The average American will buy 11 cars during a lifetime. A two-driver household will buy 22 cars during a lifetime.

By financing instead of paying cash, the average family has a gain in savings of $3662 in a 5-year period. Over a lifetime they could save $40,282. But these numbers do not consider inflation. They also do not consider the fact that most people trade in cars every 4 years, not 5.

The cost for cars will go up considerably in the next 10, 20 and 30 years. That will increase these numbers. What if interest rates go up? That will affect these numbers as well. They will all be higher.

Here is another consideration...

If you are thinking there are taxes on the savings account, you are absolutely correct. The savings account is not Politically Free. Government can increase the taxes on that account and then the profit from borrowing would be less. This would result in less MONEY, less CHOICE and less FREEDOM.

So the question becomes, how do I create Political Freedom (no taxes) for my money so it could grow and compound uninterrupted until the end of my life? That sounds like a novel idea for just a minute until you think what good is my money if I can't use it? The Financial Bunker holds the answer.

Build Your Bunker.

Chapter Eight

The Debtor, The Saver, The Wealth Creator

To appreciate the full potential of a Financial Bunker, an elementary lesson in how money works is given in this chapter. Its knowledge about how money works that should be required in every school in America.

In the penny example, we illustrated why compounding should never be allowed to reset. But how can you apply that to real life? Is it possible to compound your money every day until you die, and still have the use, the control and liquidity without resetting? Absolutely. That is one of the significant features of Bunker building. However, most people never realize the wealth potential of compounding because they don't understand how money works.

The following three scenarios unveil a basic understanding of money, with the third scenario your first introduction to Financial Bunkers. If the numbers used here seem trivial, add a zero or two to the end of them to make them more meaningful.

Profile #1 - Dave The Debtor

Dave the Debtor holds a job, but never has any money. He has no savings and because of that he earns no interest on money. He loses substantial amounts of money over his lifetime because of the interest he pays banks to borrow and finance his lifetime need for housing, cars and other capital expenditures.

Every 4 years Dave trades in his car and finances a new one. Over his lifetime he will buy 10 cars. Every car Dave buys costs him $4,482 in interest charges. If we use a historically normal loan interest rate of 7% and each car costs him $30,000 the amount of interest he will (pay) lose to banks during his lifetime is $44,820. By the way, Dave is married and he has two cars, not one. That makes his total lifetime interest lost to banks $89,640. All of this before any adjustment for rising car prices due to inflation.

1 Car - $30,000

Interest Cost = $4,482

10 Cars Interest Cost = $44,820

20 Cars Interest Cost = $89,640

Figure 9

Dave is the most profitable customer a bank could ever hope for. Not only will Dave finance cars, he will also finance his washer and dryer, stereo, boat, dental bills, vacations, and most of these will be at higher unsecured interest rates.

Dave will never get ahead because he has not yet learned how to save, and how to delay his gratification. Until he recognizes his financial behavior problem he will never accumulate any substantial amount of wealth. He loses large volumes of money during his lifetime, which diminishes his level of Freedom. Dave the Debtor retires and dies in poverty. Even if Dave dies in debt, the banks will have made more than enough money during Dave's life to cover their loss. He will be a dependent of the banking system all of his life.

Profile #2 - Suzie The Saver

Suzie The Saver has mastered saving and delaying her gratification until she has the money to buy something. She earns some interest on her money while it sits in a bank account but Suzie thinks debt is bad so she pays cash for everything. As a saver, she starts from zero and builds up a savings then takes it out and uses it to buy major consumer items. As you will see, this is a costly financial mistake.

Suzie's problem is that she suffers from Day 22 syndrome discussed in the penny-compounding example. In order to finance her life, she breaks the continuum of compounding with her savings, which resets her compounding back to zero.

Take a look at what Suzie is doing in Figure 10.

Saves $30,000
@5% Interest =$3942 (4 years)

Year 1 - $7500
Year 2 - $7500
Year 3 - $7500
Year 4 - $7500

Then Spends = $30,000

Savings Balance 40 Years Later

Before Taxes = $123,888

After Taxes = $67,213

Figure 10

Let's say that she first saves $7500 per year and every 4 years she buys a new car for $30,000. Like Dave, she will buy 10 cars over her lifetime as well.

At a historically normal savings rate of 5%, the amount of interest she will earn on her savings by saving first then paying cash over the next 40 years is $123,888. This is the result of leaving the interest in her account, and only withdrawing $30,000 every 4 years. Up to this point, Suzie seems to know what she is doing.

However, after Suzie pays taxes on her savings in just a 28% tax bracket, the after tax compounded savings results in just $67,213. This is a 50% loss of wealth accumulation and Freedom.

Also, these numbers are before any consideration that her car will cost more each time she buys one due to inflation. At the end of 40 years this is all Suzie has to show for her way of thinking.

Suzie's money is not Politically Free. She pays income taxes on her savings, which further diminishes its compounding ability. She will never become wealthy doing this because she constantly stops and restarts the compounding.

Charles The Wealth Creator

Charles creates one pool of savings with just $7500 for four years for a total of $30,000 just like Suzie. However, **he never adds any more money.** Keep in mind, Suzie must save every year in order to pay cash for her cars.

Instead of paying cash, Charles gets a loan and finances 10 cars ten times, all of them at 7 percent interest. The interest charge for each car is $4,482 His total finance charges during this 40-year period comes to $44,820.

So how did Charles finish?

Charles FINANCES his cars

10 Cars
7% Interest
48 Month Financing per car

Lifetime Interest Costs

=$44,820

Figure 11

Charles Saves $30,000 @5%
Interest =$3942 (no taxes)

Year 1 - $7500
Year 2 - $7500
Year 3 - $7500
Year 4 - $7500

Balance 40 Years Later
NO INCOME TAXES = $196,587

Figure 12

Net Gain Over Suzie

Charles Savings = $196,587
(minus)

Interest Cost = $44,820

Wealth Creation = $151,767

Figure 13

After 40 years, Charles has $196,587 in his savings. After you subtract the interest charges he paid to finance his cars of $44,820, he has $151,767 of wealth creation and Freedom.

By financing, instead of saving up and paying cash he beats Suzie "I Pay Cash" by more than 200%! Imagine if Charles was a two-car household.

How did Charles do this?

Charles has a system where he has the full use of his savings without ever resetting the compounding. In fact he has a system where his money will compound until the day he dies, not just his last car purchase. He finances all of his cars and major purchases **without using a commercial bank.** He never pays cash. And he pays no income taxes on his savings, ever. Even when Charles dies, there will be no income tax due on his savings.

When Charles chooses to retire he will do so with passive tax-free income from his plan.

Charles built a Financial Bunker.

He has the full use, control and liquidity of his money to finance the major purchases in life, **without ever stopping the compounding.** He thoroughly understands the Principles of Money.

Here is the final result of Charles' money choices…

He creates more **MONEY.**
He has more **CHOICE** because he creates more money.
He has more **FREEDOM** in his life because he has more choice.
Money = Choice = Freedom

Charles uses his Financial Bunker to grow and accumulate his money outside the control of Banks, Wall Street and Government. He has no need for traditional banking loans as he self-finances all of his major purchases. If he misses a payment, his credit score remains unaffected. In fact if he chooses to miss 3 payments, he only is responsible to himself for the accounting. He holds a checking account just for convenience. Late in his life, or when he chooses he can receive tax-free passive income from his Financial Bunker System. When he dies, all of the money inside his Financial Bunker will pass to his family income tax free.

Build Your Bunker.

Section Three

How To Build A Financial Bunker

Chapter Nine

What Is A Bunker?

If you were to show someone a chair and ask what they were looking at, they would mostly likely say a chair. However, ask a person holding a stack of books about to fall over, and for them, they see a table. Ask a painter what he sees of the chair and the painter sees a ladder. Ask the person who wishes to stop the wind from blowing the door shut and they see a door stop.

At the beginning of this book we discussed the elements of Political, Economic and Spiritual Freedom. What you are about to discover is a powerful section of the tax code that exudes those Freedoms.

It is one of the best-kept secrets and the most misunderstood aspect of how money works and what you can do with it. However, most people overlook the Freedom and power a Financial Bunker holds because like the chair, they only see a chair as something to sit on and not the other simple but powerful solutions it provides.

When people are presented with places to save their money, the most immediate question they ask is, "What is the rate of return?" Is that because we are so trained by society to immediately look at the rate of return in a financial instrument? It would seem so if you look at all of the billions of dollars lost by those who were lured in by the promise of high returns on Wall Street and other scams. In the penny compounding example we learned there are higher level considerations than just rate of return. In the context of Freedom, the most important attribute is the amount of control the Government has over one's money.

Warren Buffet pays income taxes at a rate less than his secretary. How does he do it? He knows where the Freedom lies in the income tax code. That is the secret to building and keeping immense wealth from the Government, legally. You must look to where the free air is in the thousands of pages of IRS code.

After taxes, the second most important consideration is where you want your money to reside. When people think about this, they think about the safety of their money. They also think about the potential manipulation of their money as well.

Money in currency form can only reside in three basic institutions, Banks, Wall Street, and insurance companies. The federal Government regulates two of these. Can you guess which two? If you guessed Banks and Wall Street, you are correct. Insurance companies are regulated by the 50 states with 50 different state regulators looking over their books.

Now look at the track record.

Over the last decade, which institution was a more secure place to hold money?

Banks?

There were hundreds of bank failures and billions of dollars lost there.

Wall Street? Even worse.

What about insurance companies? There is not even a statistical rounding error compared to the first two.

During the great depression insurance companies had an impressive track record of safety and security and even in the recent historic stock market crash they remained virtually undisturbed by the event. Why is this so? It's how they operate and how they are regulated.

And what about AIG? This is a common misunderstanding about insurance companies. AIG (American International Group) is an insurance holding company that owns nearly 200 separate insurance companies around the world. AIG, the holding company was one of the beneficiaries of the Government bailout during the financial crisis.

What is not mainstream knowledge and understanding about AIG is during that period, their American subsidiary American General Life Insurance Company experienced no financial issues whatsoever. In fact, insurance regulators put out bulletins to agents telling them if they replaced the insurance of the AIG subsidiary they would be investigated. The issues were with the holding company, not the subsidiary life insurance company.

If you want to build a Financial Bunker, you do it with insurance companies, specifically life insurance companies regulated by the 50 states, not the Federal Government. That is where you begin.

What you are about to discover is that life insurance can serve more than just the purpose of insuring a life. If used properly, it can create immense amounts of personal Freedom.

Build Your Bunker.

Chapter Ten

Internal Revenue Code
Section 7702

Deep within the volumes of the United States Income Tax code lies the most powerful tax Freedom that continues to survive after 100 years of tax oppression.

It's life insurance, plain and simple. It's IRS Code Section 7702. What most people understand about life insurance is limited to what they hear in the media, or mainstream financial planning. Like the chair analogy, THEY only see life insurance in one dynamic.

However for those who understand it, the financial power and control of money through this section is daunting. As you will see, those who have figured this out, have billions at work under IRS Code Section 7702 creating massive amounts of wealth, free of income taxes. Through it they are insuring their future independence for themselves, their families and their corporations.

The use of life insurance existed centuries before the tax code was published in 1913. Rather than see families become dependent and poverty stricken, life insurance was created to preserve the Freedom of surviving spouses and children upon a family member's premature death. These policies provided a death benefit with a savings element. After a number of years of paying premiums the savings equaled or exceeded the original death benefit.

When the first income tax laws were passed in 1913, congress created an income tax exemption on the cash value growth inside life insurance. They also exempted the death benefit from income taxes. This exemption remains today.

Until the emergence of individual retirements accounts in 1974 and later 401k plans, the use of a cash value life insurance policy was a common way of saving for the future, and providing the family a death benefit. At retirement, if the death benefit was no longer needed, the policy could be converted into a guaranteed stream of retirement income or income from the dividends on the policy.

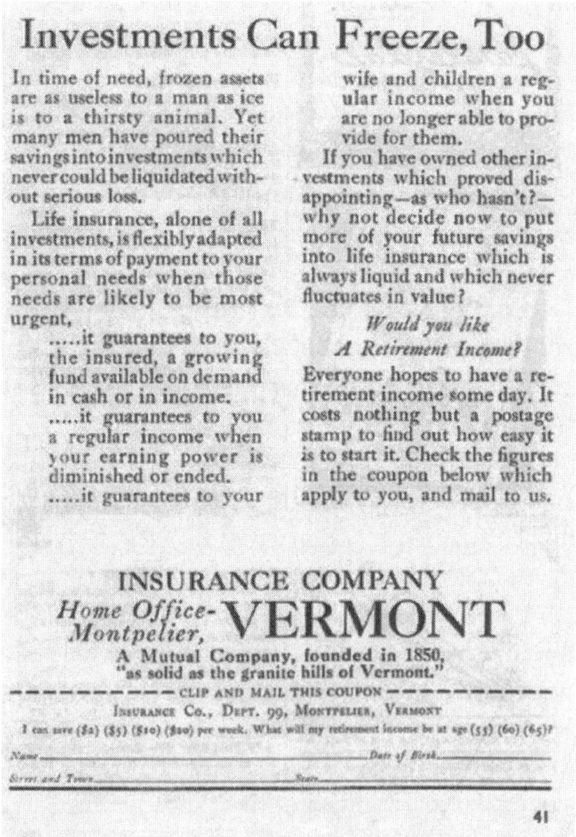

Figure 14

The stock market crash and banking failures of the 30's were an unforgettable frozen moment in the minds of Americans back then. The ad in Figure 14 from the 1930's illustrates the thinking about money even during that period. Farmers who lost money in the banks were able to take loans against their policies to keep their farms going. Thousands of Americans were able to access the cash values when they lost their jobs. Retail business owners were able to stay afloat. Because there was a contractual guarantee, there was no loss of value and the money put into these policies could be relied upon. **These plans were and still to this day are the ultimate "Financial Bunker" for money.**

What A Bunker Looks Like

In Figure 15 you can see the basic strategy for building a Financial Bunker.

You begin by creating a pool of savings using IRS Code Section 7702. Under the income tax code it is allowed to grow and compound income tax free until death. During life, you maintain the use, control and liquidity of this money through the ability to freely collateralize it without any tax consequence or explanation. At retirement or whenever your bunker is fully funded, passive tax-free income can be drawn. At death, the entire value less any loans passes to your family income tax free.

The Power Of Compounding

During life, this pool of savings can be collateralized and loans can be made against it without resetting the compounding. Loans from the insurance company can be used for any purpose and any reason without application or approval such as cars, homes, college education, business loans, or investment loans. When banks become unattractive sources of financing due to costs, rates, terms or charges, the Financial Bunker becomes the ultimate source of privatized financing to be used personally within the family, for business, or otherwise.

Once money is inside the Financial Bunker it is completely emancipated from the income tax system until the day you die. It holds the key to uninterrupted financial compounding and the ability to create passive income that is free from taxes. You have created a system of Political, Economic and Spiritual Freedom with your money that you can enjoy all during your life, and a system for your children and grandchildren as well.

The Financial Bunker is Thomas Jefferson's answer to the question "How does one maintain Freedom in a world where one's Freedom is controlled through money?"

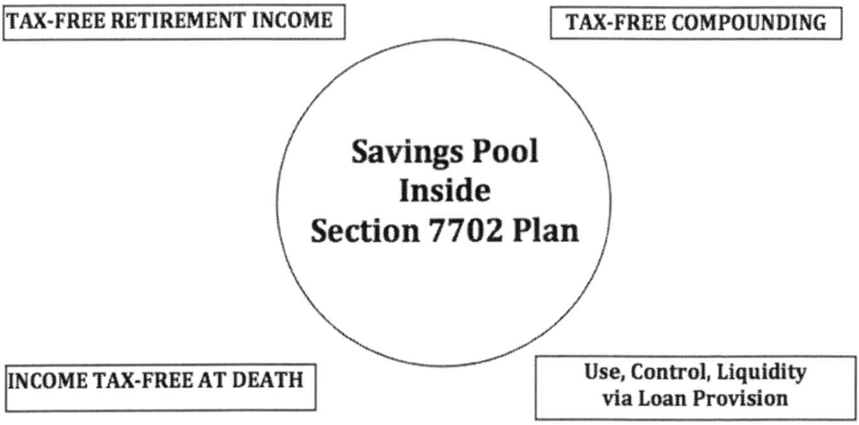

Figure 15

So why is this thinking not prevalent today?

Answer: changes in tax laws.

In 1974, Congress under the influence of Wall Street manipulated the money of Americans through taxes to take it from safe places such as life insurance and put it into IRAs and 401k plans. We moved away from a "Bunker system", one of self-reliance, to one of dependence as discussed earlier with the triangle.

A small number of insurance companies continued to market these plans and today, after the crash of the stock market, after the failure of the banking system and now with the advent of the coming wave of taxes, these plans are being rediscovered. However, you will not find them marketed by the traditional life insurance agent or financial planner. A Financial Bunker is a specially designed policy that requires extensive training and understanding. To help you understand life insurance better, let's review the different types and risks each one may hold.

Types Of Life Insurance

Even professional life insurance agents can find life insurance confusing.

There is a difference between building a Bunker and just buying life insurance.

The basic elements of life insurance begin with a legal contract and a premium payment in return for a future death benefit. After that there are two basic types of life insurance, Term insurance and Permanent insurance. The distinction between these is critical as only one of these is a true "Financial Bunker."

Term Insurance

The first option is that you can choose to pay just the actuarial amount of insurance also called mortality cost for your age and health that would be due if you died today.

Term gives you the maximum amount of coverage for the least amount of money at the moment you buy it. There is no savings element. If you do not die before your actuarial life expectancy, the cost of owning these policies becomes prohibitive near the end of your life. Quite simply, the older you get the closer you get to dying when the premiums are the highest.

Nearly all term life insurance policies lapse without a death claim paid after years of paying the premiums. The reason is that people simply can't afford the rising premiums when they get older. It is the most profitable life insurance product that exists and just for that reason. **This is not a Financial Bunker.**

Permanent Insurance

Permanent life insurance exists to be the policy you hold until the day you die. All forms of this come from the original "Bunker" policies known as whole life policies which include a savings element.

There are four variations of permanent life insurance policies. The first three create a savings element combined with term insurance. These policies provide protection as long as the savings grows as projected. "Grows as projected" is the critical consideration of these policies and the reason many have failed. The last and fourth plan is the "Bunker".

Universal Life (UL)

Universal Life is known as (UL). Within a UL policy there is a savings element that earns interest and is connected to a term insurance policy where the costs of the term insurance are deducted from the savings element. The approach is that the savings will grow over time so when the term insurance costs that are deducted from the savings rise, there will be enough savings to cover the costs.

The success of UL is based on current interest rates. Many of these policies were purchased in the 1980's when interest rates were very high. Illustrations of these policies assumed rates would stay high. Since that time, these have been a disappointment as policyholders received notices to either pay additional premiums or their policies will lapse without a death benefit. Most people choose to lapse or substantially reduce the death benefit to keep the policy in force at current interest rates. **This is not a Financial Bunker.**

Variable Universal Life (VUL)

The second type of life insurance with a savings element is called Variable Universal Life, or VUL. In these plans the savings element is invested in mutual funds. Like the UL, the goal is to grow the cash value in order to sustain the policy until death while term insurance costs are deducted from the savings. Policy owners who purchased these policies were also disappointed during the last decade when substantial losses occurred in the stock market.

Those who purchased VUL in the 1990's thought their savings element in mutual funds would continue its rise. As a result of the savings losses, the prohibitive term insurance costs deducted out of these policies caused many of them to lapse. **This is not a Financial Bunker.**

Indexed Universal Life (IUL)

The third type of life insurance with a savings element is called Indexed Universal Life, or IUL. Like the previous two, IUL uses a savings element attached to a term insurance policy. However, with IUL the savings element is not invested in the stock market, nor is the rate of return based on interest rates.

The savings of an IUL policy grows through interest earned using a method called index crediting. Index interest crediting works by taking a measurement of data points in the financial markets.

With IUL, there can be losses in the cash value accumulations. The reason for the potential loss is the charges for the term insurance (mortality costs) must come out of your savings. This creates the possibility of lapsing where the policy is not in force when you die. Additionally, IUL cannot operate without uninterrupted compounding until the day you die. Should the policy not credit interest in a particular year, there would be no compounding and a year's worth of compounding is lost. That is time that cannot be replaced.

Because of the uncertainty about Wall Street returns, and the possibility of a loss in any given year, IUL carries risk and uncertainty as to the viability of the death benefit late in life. IUL is complex. It requires monitoring and management of the accumulation process with regard to the variety of indexing options and methods. The ultimate responsibility of all of this lies with the policyholder. **This is not a Financial Bunker.**

Whole Life Insurance (WL) - The Bunker

Finally the last type of life insurance is the one used to build Financial Bunkers. This form of life insurance is the oldest, most secure, and most proven based on the accumulated history of how money works in America.

It is known as dividend paying whole life insurance. Whole life insurance is not exciting. It does not have the allure and excitement of Wall Street. However, those who appreciate its attributes of compounding and the life enhancing simplicity of its contractual guarantees, realize it is the most powerful, and most secure wealth protection vehicle that exists. In the next chapter you will understand why. **This IS The Financial Bunker.**

Build Your Bunker.

Chapter Eleven

The Jet Engine Of Financial Compounding

If you fly commercially today, most likely you will take a plane that has jet engines. The reason for this is that the jet engine has become the most reliable and most efficient form of propulsion known in aviation today. But what makes it so?

Simplicity.

To understand why a jet engine is more reliable, we need to compare it to the internal combustion engine, the one typically used for propeller planes.

The traditional internal combustion engine is complex. It has dozens of parts moving at different speeds creating massive amounts of opposing kinetic energy, vibration, and wear. The success of that engine is dependent upon the integrity of all those parts. Failure of any one of these can cause engine failure.

A jet engine on the other hand is simple. It has only one moving part. That part is a perfectly balanced wheel with fan blades. The fan blades suck air into a chamber where it is mixed with jet fuel and then expelled out with tremendous force. The simplicity of this propulsion process with its one moving part, and its historical demonstration of safety is why the jet engine is the engine of choice for commercial aviation.

Now let's review Whole Life insurance and why it is the financial engine of choice for building a Financial Bunker.

The Power Of Simplicity

There are two elements that make up the basic essence of a whole life insurance policy: money and dividends. The more money you put inside of the policy, the more dividends you will earn, it's that simple. There are no ongoing fees or charges deducted out of the cash values after dividends are paid. There is no dependency on Wall Street to go up.

A Financial Compounding Machine

Remember the compounding example using the penny from the earlier chapter? A whole life insurance policy is a financial compounding machine.

Whole life insurance pays dividends and when used in a properly structured Bunker policy, the dividends compound undisturbed until the day you die. This means that you never reset the compounding of money, ever! You have the full use, control and liquidity of money, without interrupting the compounding of the dividends. A whole life insurance policy used carefully can protect compounding, and do it your entire life without income taxes.

The creation of whole life came from a time in America where Freedom and government bondage were well understood by everyone. Today, the creation of a Financial Bunker using whole life insurance holds the key to Freedom; Politically, Economically, and Spiritually.

Rate Of Return

The rate of return and the dividends paid on the money you place in the policy will be determined by three factors: interest rates, mortality experience and the operating costs of the insurance company. Insurance companies invest money in bonds. As interest rates move up, the rate of return on their portfolio goes up and the dividends can go up. The mortality experience of a company, that being how many policyholders were projected to die versus actual deaths affects profitability. Finally, operating expenses. Did they go up or down or stay the same. The latter two factors are generally very predictable. So what ultimately determines rate of return in a dividend paying whole life insurance policy? Interest rates.

When interest rates go down the rates of return go down, when interest rates go up, the rates of return go up. It's very simple. On average, the historical industry rates of return on Financial Bunker policies range from 4 to 6 percent. If that does not seem high, remember that this is a Financial Bunker, not an investment. It is a rock solid place for money to reside income tax-free while you deploy it income tax-free into investments and other uses.

Predictability

Mutual life insurance companies have a history of paying dividends without interruption for over 100 years. Dividends are a predictable stream of income. And while they are compounding, the dividends go up year, after year, after year.

Think about that as it relates to putting a value on a business. One key factor in determining the dollar value of a business is a predictable stream of income. Does the business earn a profit one year, and a loss the next year? Is there a radical change up and down in profits every other year? Or, does the business create a profit every year with a predictability that the profits will increase year after year?

That is exactly what a dividend paying whole life insurance policy is all about. After decades of compounding, a substantial amount of money can be accumulated late in life when the highest degree of predictability in income is required.

Mutual Life Insurance Companies vs. Stock Life Insurance Companies

To build your Bunker with whole life insurance, you must understand that there are two types of life insurance companies, mutual and stock companies.

The fundamental difference between the two is that one acts in the best interest of their policyholders, and one acts in the best interest of their stockholders. Mutual insurance companies return their profits back to the policyholders in the form of a dividend because the policyholders are the mutual insurance company's owners. They act in the best interest of the policyholder.

Mutual Insurance Companies

- **Owned by policyholders**
- **Pay profits to policyholders**
- **In business to serve policyholders**

Stock Insurance Companies

- **Owned by stockholders**
- **Pay profits to stockholders**
- **In business to make stock value go up**

Figure 16

The company's operating costs, how many claims were made, and the interest earned on the investment portfolio determines dividends. In a rising interest rate environment these companies can increase their dividends. In a declining interest rate environment one would expect to see decreases. Keep in mind the time continuum for compounding the money in your Bunker is the rest of your life.

Stock companies that offer whole life insurance differ from mutual companies in that their profits go to their stockholders, not the policyholders. It is in their best interest to keep the stockholders happy at all times or the price of the company stock will go down. Conflicts of interest can occur at stock companies. If the senior management of a stock insurance company is compensated in shares of stock, it's possible that the management could make decisions in the best interest of themselves, instead of policyholders.

This differentiation is especially important today as many Wall Street firms have recently purchased life insurance companies with the intention of skimming from policyholders just like fees charged on 401k plans.

Loans - Economic Freedom Of Your Money

Why take a loan instead of a withdrawal? If you remember the lesson from Charles the wealth creator, he borrowed against his policy, which avoided the interruption of compounding. This allowed him to take advantage of the power of compounding until the day he died. He enjoys the use, control and liquidity of his money through this feature.

Once you have made your first premium payment, the insurance company will make you a loan against the cash value inside. You are not borrowing money out of the policy, but merely receiving a loan from the insurance company who takes money out of their general fund. This process is nearly identical to what banks do when a loan is made against a time deposit. However, there are dramatic differences.

A loan from a whole life policy can be made for any purpose with just a signature of the policy owner. There is no loan application. Typically funds can be received within 7 days when linked to a bank account. If you miss a payment, nobody will come and repossess your property. You even have flexibility as to how you want to repay, if you ever repay. Some people never repay the loan against the policy and when they die, it is subtracted from the death benefit. When a loan is taken the insurance company does charge interest but remember the bankers math from Chapter Seven? While your money is compounding inside the policy you earn interest on it even when you have a loan against it.

Many Americans who understand the full utility of a Financial Bunker make it their complete source of financing. They prefer to borrow from their Bunker instead of going to the bank, filling out an application and waiting for the bank's loan approval. Furthermore, those who are especially concerned about the injustices of fractional reserve banking realize that the mere signature on a new loan from a bank, causes inflation.

The Contract - Spiritual Freedom

When purchasing a policy from a life insurance company you have a contract. Everything about the policy is in writing. You are presented with what the minimum guarantees are and what your rights and privileges are as the contract owner. You know in advance what to expect from the policy.

There is no market risk so there is **no possibility of loss** due to Wall Street market fluctuations. All life insurance companies hold financial ratings. These are A.M. Best, Standard and Poor's, Fitch, Moody's and Comdex. You know the quality of the company by their ratings. The higher the ratings, the greater the Spiritual Freedom you will hold. You decide.

Proper Structure Of A Financial Bunker Policy

Now that you understand we use a dividend paying whole life insurance policy from a mutual insurer to build a Bunker, you must also understand that it is not built with just any whole life policy. A financial Bunker is **a specially designed policy** created for high cash value accumulation, not for the death benefit.

We are building Bunkers for the safe accumulation of money, tax-free supplemental income, additional medical indemnity when available, wealth transfer, and a private source of hassle-free personal financing.

Financial Bunker - Tax-Free Attributes

We want to protect the ability to use the money from the Bunker for financing purposes and for future income without creating any taxes. The policy must be built correctly from an income tax standpoint, so that any loans against the policy will not be considered taxable distributions to the IRS. An agent without this training will build a policy that does not conform to the IRS regulations for tax-free loans. You want your Financial Bunker to provide for the use, control and liquidity of your money through withdrawals and loans **without income taxes.** To do this you cannot dump all the money in at once. Funding takes place over a number of years.

Tax-Free Income

At a point in time where you have enough money built up in the policy, tax-free income can be created through several options. The first is to have the dividends of the policy paid out in cash. The second option would be to withdraw money directly from the policy income tax-free until reaching the gains. In both of these cases, the withdrawal of this money is income tax-free because it is considered a return of your original principal.

Gains in the policy are taken out through income tax-free loans. At death, the loan is subtracted from the death benefit and the proceeds are paid out income tax-free. Those who are older in life and desire additional income find this option an attractive way to supplement their lifestyle without increasing their overall tax bracket.

Funding Strategy

For the purpose of illustration we build Bunkers over 10 year periods with the objective of getting as much money "in" over that 10 years.

$100,000 Bunker

Year 1 $10,000
Year 2 $10,000
Year 3 $10,000
Year 4 $10,000
Year 5 $10,000
Year 6 $10,000
Year 7 $10,000
Year 8 $10,000
Year 9 $10,000
Year 10 $10,000

$100,000

Figure 17

The first question to be answered is what is the size of the Financial Bunker you would like to build? Once you know the answer to that question, then you know how to build the bunker.

Let's say you want a $100,000 Bunker. To build a Financial Bunker with the attributes discussed here you would fund it over a 10-year period with $10,000 each year. Based on your age, health condition and dividend rate by the time you reach the tenth year you will have fully funded your Financial Bunker.

If you want to build a one million dollar bunker you would fund it with $100,000 over a 10-year period. A 10 million dollar bunker, you would fund with one million dollars a year and so on. During and after completion of the funding, the money and all the growth inside the policy is completely emancipated from income taxes as long as it stays there. If you close it out and take your money in the future, you will give up your Freedom, and you would owe income taxes on the gains. Die owning your Financial Bunker, and you created immense Freedom for your family.

Illustrations

To see exactly what the projected cash value growth, death benefits and tax-free income possibilities are you must get an illustration from a licensed life insurance agent. As mentioned previously, agents who thoroughly understand Financial Bunker building are rare.

To find an agent who is an expert on building Financial Bunkers go to **www.BuildYourBunker.com/HELP**.

Through this you will be referred to a licensed professional who will provide a personalized illustration designed for the specific Financial Bunker you wish to create for yourself. It will show year by year how money can compound, how you can take loans, and what the death benefits are. Whether you start small or start big, just start. Someday, the Government will say you can no longer build Financial Bunkers. Those who built Bunkers will most likely be "grandfathered" and get to keep them.

Those who waited will lose out. Act now. Time is money and your Freedom.

Build Your Bunker.

Chapter Twelve

The Secret About Banks THEY Don't Want Us To Know

What are **Wells Fargo, Bank Of America, JP Morgan Chase Bank** and dozens of others hiding from Americans? It's that THEY are the single largest consumers of cash value life insurance. It is hard to believe, but banks use significant amounts of their customer's money to purchase life insurance.

The numbers are not easily attained but according to the Wall Street Journal, as of 2008 commercial banks held over 122.3 billion dollars in cash value life insurance policies.

Here is a brief listing of selected banks and the amounts held in bank owned life insurance policies during this period, according to the research published by the Wall Street Journal May 9, 2009.

Citigroup	**4.2 billion**
Bank of America	**17.3 billion**
JP Morgan Chase	**11.1 billion**
Wells Fargo	**17.7 billion**

The question is…why would a bank do such a thing?

Well it turns out, that banks understand the significant Freedoms that cash value life insurance holds and they use those Freedoms to maintain the profitability in their business now and in the future. In essence, they are using life insurance to insure their future existence. Here is how they do it.

Banks take in deposits from customers to create profits by loaning that money out. A portion of those profits and deposits are used to purchase cash value life insurance on the lives of the management of the bank. During the time the money sits in the policy, the bank enjoys the same Political Freedom as an individual would.

Banks pay no income taxes on the gains earned on money held in the policy. When a death of one of the bank's employees occurs, the policy pays a death benefit to the bank, income tax-free; more Political Freedom. Now take a look at what life insurance does to empower banks.

Tier 1 Operating Capital

Because cash value life insurance is contractual, certain, and uses compounding without resetting, and because it holds all the Freedoms we as individuals would desire for ourselves, cash value life insurance meets the requirements to serve as a Tier 1 asset for banks.

Tier 1 assets make up the safest money and investments that a bank is required to maintain in order to operate under the banking laws of America. Simply put, cash value life insurance is one of the safest places money can reside on the planet and the Government says banks can and should use cash value life insurance as part of their operating capital.

What is ironic is that in some cases, the bank owned life insurance policies were the best performing asset of the bank during the financial crisis. Because the Government Comptroller of the Currency says banks can hold up to 25% of their Tier 1 money in cash value life insurance, most take good advantage and stock up with as much as they can. And remember, this money comes from the depositors and bank profits! Think about what you just read when someone tells you permanent cash value life insurance is not a good choice.

Disneyland

When the founders of America used the terms Life, Liberty and The Pursuit of Happiness they had no idea of what America was to become, nor the inspiration those words might have on future Americans. But it was through the Freedoms exuded by cash value whole life insurance that the happiest place on earth came to be, Disneyland.

As the story goes from Walt Disney's biography, Walt approached bankers to get help for the financing of Disneyland. Now imagine Walt walking into the bank and telling the bankers that he wanted to buy an orange grove way outside of the city and put an amusement park on it. Walt's brother thought it was a ridiculous idea, and even laughed at the idea of charging people money for this. The bankers rejected Walt's idea. Through the Freedom found in Walt's cash value whole life policy he took a loan to finance the project. Think about that for a moment.

If it were not for the existence and Freedom created by the accumulation of money within a whole life policy, Disneyland, and the multi-billion dollar Disney Corporation, which owns ABC and many other businesses might not exist today. Think of all the wealth that was created because Walt had the forethought to build a savings inside a whole life policy where it held Political, Financial and Spiritual Freedom. Walt was also 29 years old when the stock market crashed in the great depression. He clearly understood at that time what could happen to money on Wall Street.

Pampered Chef

In the basement of her home Doris Christopher started a party business of kitchen tools, food products and cookbooks. Through this she created a company with a direct sales force of over 60,000 representatives. She founded the company Pampered

Chef with a loan from her whole life insurance policy for $3,000. She later sold the company to Warren Buffet for more than a billion dollars.

McDonalds

During the early years Ray Kroc was financially challenged to keep McDonalds going. Initially he had trouble figuring out how to make money through franchising. Eventually he settled on the correct formula. But during this early period he needed money to keep the business floating. He resorted to borrowing from his whole life insurance policies to help cover the salaries of his employees. Today McDonalds is one of the most recognized brand names in the world with over 30,000 stores.

J.C. Penney

As a young man in 1898 James Cash Penney was such a hard working employee that owners of a small chain of dry goods stores offered him a partnership. This led to a series of expanded store openings across the country, which Penney was the sole owner of. By 1929, he had 1400 stores. When the stock market crash came in 1929, the depression and crash took its toll on Penney's empire. Fortunately he was able to keep the company afloat through a loan from his whole life insurance policies. It should be noted that during the great depression, life insurance cash values and gold were the two main storage places for value that people could count on.

Foster Farms

If you buy chicken from a grocery store, or eat chicken at a restaurant there is a good chance it comes from Foster Farms, one of the largest producers of poultry in the world. In 1939 Max and Verda Foster started their business by borrowing $1,000 against their whole life cash value life insurance policy. Today they have over 10,000 employees and provide fresh, all-natural chicken free of preservatives, and other additives to retailers and restaurants throughout the world.

Build Your Bunker.

Section Four

Financial Designs For Freedom

Now that you have an understanding of why you need to Build Your Bunker, and you understand the structure of a basic Bunker, let's take a look at what a Bunker can do for you. In this section we have compiled a variety of **"Bunker Strategies"**, from simple to complex Bunker planning. You will realize that the more money you can get into a Bunker, the more Freedom, as defined by the formula Money=Choice=Freedom you will achieve for yourself and others.

It's important to note that this is not a complete listing of all possible Bunker strategies. When you add in the possibility of using trusts, estate exemptions, making loans from trusts using Bunker money, the possibilities are endless. Who knows, you just might become the next billionaire like Walt Disney because you had a Bunker when opportunity presented itself. If you ever speak to someone who has already built a Bunker, they will most likely say opportunity <u>did</u> present itself and they capitalized on that because of their Bunker.

Bunker Strategy #1

College Education Funding

Why

Bill and Martha age 70 are the grandparents of 3-year old Sharon and want a substantial college fund for Sharon when she is ready. As they look around at the millions of college graduates who are in debt to the Government, they are determined to protect her from that. When looking at the typical state college funding plans, they do not want the risk of the Government's 529 savings plans that use mutual funds.

They want something that is certain, a plan with guarantees. They also want to make sure that if something happens to Sharon's father, Sharon will have enough money to fall back on. They understand that everything is financed and that you either give up, or pay interest when you make purchases. Bill and Martha don't want their children to be in debt to the Government, or banks.

How It Works

The grandparents control and fund a Bunker with $20,000 a year for the next 10 years. This will be the source of funding for their granddaughter's college fund. Although the grandparents could insure themselves with the death benefit, they chose their son (age 30) as the insured to allow the money in the Bunker to compound with the longest possible time period. The grandparents are the owners and beneficiaries of the policy. After 10 years, they have a financial Bunker with over $200,000 that will grow and compound until the day their son dies. Upon the death of the grandparents, the ownership of the policy transfers to their son.

When their granddaughter goes to college, they will take a loan against the policy to finance Sharon's college education 15 years later when she goes to college. Bill and Martha have an agreement with their son who will pay back the loan to the Bunker policy at an agreed upon interest rate and time period. The son will inherit other assets when his parents die and will refill (pay back the loan) using those assets. At that time, the Bunker policy will transfer to the son who will have the full use, control and liquidity of the money during his life.

Bunker #1 – Grandparents Funding College

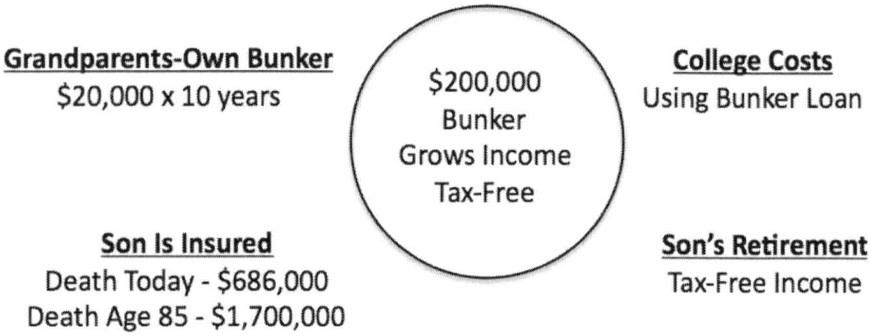

Figure 18

What The Bunker Does

- The Grandparents have insured the future care and security of their granddaughter. With the payment of the first $20,000, an immediate benefit is created of $686,000 payable to the grandparents upon the son's death
- Through the loan provision of the policy the grandparents can loan their son the cost of college estimated at $50,000 a year for a total of $200,000
- When the daughter is age 18, the son will be age 45. By that time his earning power is higher allowing the son to

repay the loan made from the Financial Bunker created by his parents more easily

- The existence of the loan through the grandparents eliminates the possibility of their granddaughter becoming a dependent of banks, or high interest student loans
- All money in the policy compounds tax-free and the loan is not taxable
- Many grants and college stipends require the demonstration of financial need. The loan from the Financial Bunker does not appear on the FAFSA college loan application protecting the opportunity for the granddaughter to be eligible for grants or awards
- By financing instead of paying cash for college, the compounding of money within the Financial Bunker is never reset and compounds until the day the son dies
- When the grandparents die, the son will become the new owner of the Bunker and can use it to finance other projects besides college funding
- At son's actuarial death of age 85 the Financial Bunker his parents built to pay for his daughter's college education pays nearly 1.7 million dollars of Politically free (tax-free) income to his family

Bunker Strategy #2

Private Family Banking

Why

John and Susan Smith want to build a Bunker to create a pool of savings for personal financing. They understand that it is better to finance than to pay cash. They want to become fully independent of banks when it comes to financing the major purchases of life. They don't want to be in debt to a bank. They realize that if they lost their job, or were unable to work for any reason, and could not make their mortgage payments, the bank would foreclose. John and Susan build a Bunker to create their own private family banking system.

How It Works

John and Susan build a Bunker putting $25,000 a year into a specially designed Bunker policy. They make John the insured since he is the higher wage earner. After 10 years they will have built up $250,000 in their financial Bunker. During this time they have been making payments for their home and have paid it down to the point where they can take a loan against their financial Bunker and pay off the mortgage to the bank. Now instead of making payments to the bank, they make payments to their financial Bunker.

Bunker #2 – Private Family Banking

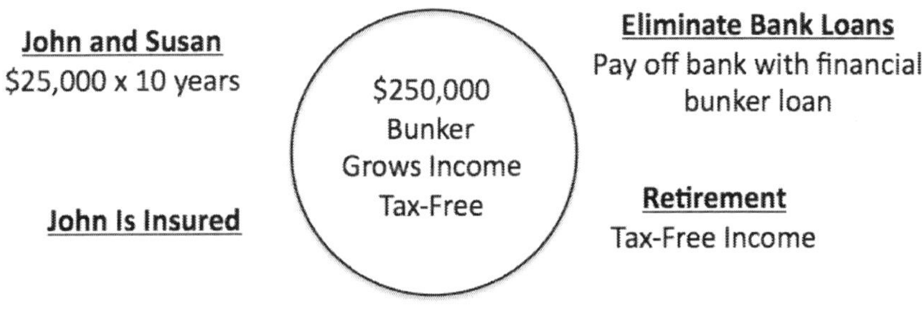

Figure 19

What The Bunker Does

- John and Susan will have built up a pool of savings where they have the use, control and liquidity of their money without resetting the compounding until the day John dies
- All money inside the Bunker compounds income tax free until John's death
- When they borrow from their Financial Bunker policies to finance their purchases, each loan repayment that pays back the loan allows them to borrow out more for new loans. This is something banks don't typically offer on installment loans
- There is no strict repayment schedule. If they lose their job they can miss payments, and possibly not pay back the loan for several years.
- There is no application or approval to get a loan from their financial Bunker policy
- At retirement, they can draw passive supplemental income that is tax-free
- When John dies, the income tax-free death benefit is paid from the policy

Bunker Strategy #3

Passive Tax-Free Retirement Income

Why

Bill is a corporate executive age 50 with a 3 million dollar stock portfolio of which 2 million is in a tax-deferred qualified retirement plan. He recognizes the risks of financial markets and wants to diversify. He also believes that taxes are going to be higher in the future and wants the ability to create additional passive tax-free income. To protect himself and his wife for the future, he builds a Bunker.

How It Works

Bill builds a 1 million dollar Bunker by funding it with $100,000 for the next 10 years using the money he has outside of his retirement plan. Should he die prematurely, the transfer of the first $100,000 creates an immediate death benefit of $1,700,000. By age 70 he has $1,618,000 in cash values and $2,617,000 in an income tax-free death benefit. At age 85 he has $3,000,000 in cash values and $3,500,000 of income tax-free death benefit.

Bunker #3 – Passive Tax-Free Retirement Income

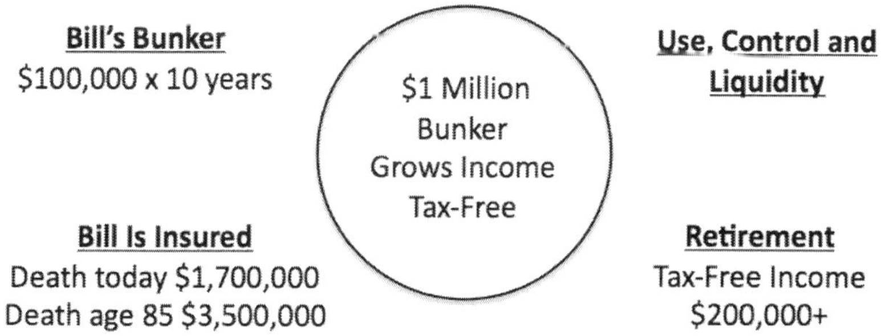

Figure 20

What The Bunker Does

- Through the creation of a financial Bunker, Bill has protected his family and his Freedom should his retirement portfolio invested on Wall Street go bust
- If he dies before his wife, his Bunker will provide a substantial supplement, income tax-free to his wife. At Bill's actuarial age of death, 85 the death benefit is $3.5 million income tax-free
- Bill anticipates that income taxes will go up. In consideration of higher taxes, he spends down his qualified retirement plan faster and then supplements it with tax-free income from his Bunker policy at age 85. At that time he withdraws $200,000 annually income tax-free. This is equivalent to $285,000 in a 30% marginal tax bracket
- At any time during the period the policy is in force, Bill also has the ability to borrow from his Bunker should an opportunity arise
- Assuming Bill spends down his qualified retirement plan and both he and his wife die in their mid 80's, he can leave his family an income tax-free inheritance instead of one that is fully taxable

Bunker Strategy #4

Real Estate Investors

Why

Jim is a 60-year-old entrepreneurial real estate developer and broker. He builds houses and apartment complexes then sells them. In order to finance his projects he must apply to banks for a loan or find other partners. Jim has substantial amounts of cash available to help with the funding of his projects, however when he uses this money he resets the compounding of his money. In addition, his cash is earning almost nothing and he pays income taxes on what he earns. Jim chooses to take his cash and build a Bunker.

How It Works

Jim decides to build a 3 million dollar Bunker with money sitting in the bank. Over the next 10 years, Jim puts $300,000 a year into a policy where he is the insured and his wife is the beneficiary. With the first $300,000 he immediately creates $3.6 million in death benefit. With each premium payment into his Bunker policy, his borrowing capacity increases to where it easily exceeds the 3 million he has put into the policy.

Jim then sets up a loan agreement between himself and his corporation. He loans money to his corporation by borrowing against his Financial Bunker policy. He charges his corporation the interest rate the corporation would have to pay for an unsecured line of credit Jim would pay in the market today. The corporation then pays Jim interest and principal back for the loan Jim made the corporation. The interest cost to the corporation is tax deductible and the net interest gain to Jim personally is considered taxable income to Jim.

What The Bunker Does

- Jim creates wealth not only in his real estate business but he puts his savings to work where he can grow and compound his money without resetting, income tax free

Bunker #4 – Real Estate Investors

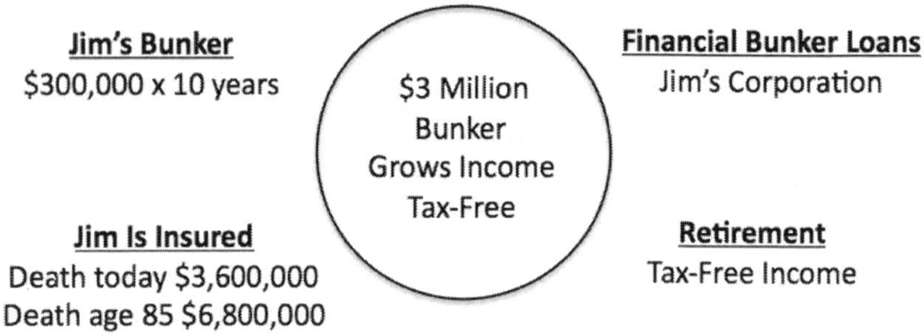

Figure 21

- Because Jim has the use, control and liquidity of money in his Financial Bunker, he has created a private loan facility to make loans to not only himself, but possibly to other real estate projects, or his own personal real estate portfolio and his corporation
- There are no credit applications or approvals required to take a loan
- Through the repayment of the loans back into his policy, he increases his borrowing capacity to make new loans, unlike a typical bank loan
- At any time, Jim can choose to turn on the income potential of his Bunker and start receiving money, income tax-free
- Upon Jim's death, his Financial Bunker policy pays a death benefit to his family income tax-free

Bunker Strategy #5

Municipal Bond Investors

Why

Carl is retired at 65 and has an investment portfolio of 40 million dollars, of which 10 million is in long-term, laddered tax-free municipal bonds. He currently is reinvesting the municipal bond interest and has no need for the income as he receives a sizeable pension. He believes interest rates will rise over the next 20 years and is concerned about the market risk of his bond portfolio over that time period.

Carl is also concerned about protecting and preserving his wealth for his wife and children. He recognizes at his actuarial age of death 85 his municipal bond portfolio could realize substantial losses in value should interest rates rise over the next 20 years. If that happens he will leave his family a bond portfolio of 6 to 7 million dollars, which is a 30 percent loss below its current par value of 10 million. Also, the yield on his portfolio at that time could be much lower than what current bond yields. Instead of leaving the value of his portfolio and wealth to chance, Carl builds a Bunker.

How It Works

Over the next 10 years Carl transfers 1 million dollars a year from his municipal bond portfolio to build a Bunker. On the first 1 million transferred into the Bunker policy, there is an immediate death benefit of $10,400,000. By year 10 he will have in excess of 10 million dollars accumulated inside his Bunker Policy. At his actuarial age of death, age 85 the death benefit is $18,000,000, all income tax free.

Bunker #5 – Municipal Bond Investors

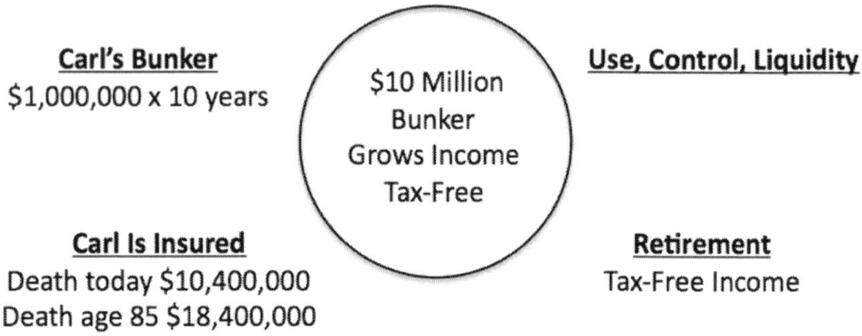

Figure 22

What The Bunker Does

- Carl gains peace of mind by eliminating the market risk from his portfolio
- Should Carl die prematurely, the initial premium provides significant additional income tax-free money to his family to reinvest and buy additional new tax-free bonds
- At 85 his actuarial age of death, his Bunker Policy provides his family with an income tax-free check in the amount of $18,400,000
- Instead of inheriting a bond portfolio that is substantially below par value, his family receives the death benefit proceeds income tax-free and purchases a brand new bond portfolio at par
- Should Carl choose, he can create tax-free income from his Bunker Policy in the future through withdrawals and loans

Bunker Strategy #6

Family (Multi-Generational) Bunker Building

Why

The Childers family wants to incorporate Financial Bunkers into their children and grandchildren's understanding of money. They believe in the Freedom that Bunker building provides and want to create independence for themselves and future generations. They understand the financial principles of Bunkers and wish to take advantage of all of the complete financial independence Financial Bunkers provide. Ultimately they want to create a system of Bunkers that can roll income tax-free from one generation to the next.

How It Works

Grandfather Bill who is age 75 wants to build a Bunker with his retirement savings. He does not need the income and wants to pass the money along to his son when he dies. While Bill is alive, he wants as much liquidity as possible in his policy, so he purchases a specially designed Bunker policy to allow for the maximum amount of cash value, instead of the maximum death benefit. This way he can still make loans from the policy, create additional tax-free income in the future, and retain control of his money.

John is Bill's son and he is 50 years old. John is a successful business owner and recognizes the wealth creation and Freedom aspects of a Financial Bunker. John has built his own Bunker and uses it to finance his business equipment, real estate and his children's college educations.

John built his Bunker with the purpose of someday being able to draw passive tax-free income in retirement. Because John and his father Bill have discussed family Bunker building, John knows that he will inherit his father's Bunker. When that day comes, John will receive the Bunker income tax-free and at that time he will roll that into his own Bunker policy and pay off the loans.

Corey, age 25 is John's son, and Bill's grandson. When Corey was 5 years old his father started a Bunker for him. Corey now uses that Bunker to get started in life by financing his first car without the need for a bank loan. Corey has set up a financing schedule and pays the loans back to his Bunker. Through this process, his father has taught him how money works and the principles of banking few children or adults ever understand.

What The Bunker Does

- When planning multi-generationally, future generations can coordinate the receipt of previous generations Financial Bunkers, (the death benefit) to fill up the policies where loans exist
- At grandfather's death, John receives the death benefit from his father's Bunker. John then rolls that money into his own Bunker to pay off the loans he holds against it
- Because the rollover from his father was strategically planned, John confidently borrowed against his Bunker for financing purposes knowing that he would fill it back up when his father died
- John can now use his Bunker to draw tax-free income from later in his life, or just leave the money to grow and compound along with the death benefit
- Upon John's death, his son Corey will do the same. Corey will receive his father's income tax-free Bunker and use the money to pay off and refill his own Bunker. Corey will then start new Bunkers for his own children.

3 Generations Of Bunker Building

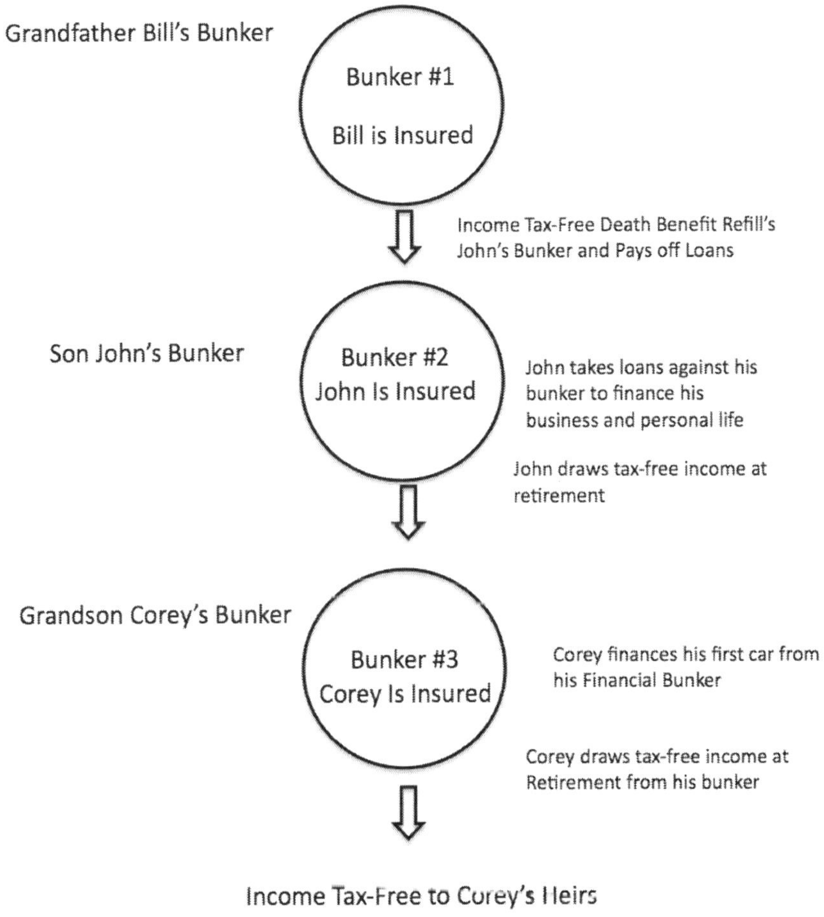

Figure 23

Through creation and strategic planning, multiple generations can escape the future income taxation of money, while retaining the use, control and liquidity to create income, or finance their lives

Families across America, who have discovered this system of wealth management and transfer, have created a dozen or more Bunker policies between family members. They understand the direct connection between Freedom and money and want to protect and preserve their Freedom for themselves and their children.

The possibilities of Bunker building across generations are too numerous to illustrate here. The purpose of this book is to open one's eyes to the possibilities of how to transfer Freedom from one generation to the next. How much, how you design it, and how you use it is up to you.

Whatever you do...

Build Your Bunker.

Section Five

Build Your Bunker-Get Started

Now you have the knowledge of why Financial Bunkers are important, what they are and how they work, the next step is to build one for yourself. You need to find a licensed life insurance professional who is an expert in this area to help you. As mentioned earlier, the typical agent does not hold the necessary knowledge of taxes and life insurance to build policies the way you need it built.

Find A Professional

At **www.BuildYourBunker.com/HELP** you can find professionals who are trained in building Financial Bunkers exactly like you have discovered here. They already understand why you want a bunker, and will strategize with you to accomplish the financial independence you set as a goal.

Determine Your Bunker Size

When you get to the end of the funding period, how big do you want your bunker to be? You pick the number. Then from that point, everything works backwards as to how you want to fund it. Some people find that after a few years, they want to put more money into their Bunker. To do that, they start another policy. Remember, the more money you get into the policy, the more financial independence you create for yourself. Because of the continued compounding of the policy, when it comes to self-financing, the amount you can borrow continues to go up every year just from the increased compounding! All without taking any more risk. This is true liberation.

Get An Illustration

When you work with a professional who is experienced with building Financial Bunkers, one of the pieces of information you will receive is the illustration. A licensed professional will provide you with a customized illustration based on your age, and the amount that you will fund your Bunker with each year. Because you are purchasing a life insurance policy, you also will need to take a medical exam and qualify. If for some reason, you can't qualify, you can still build a Bunker by putting the death benefit on another family member. This is quite common especially with older people.

Get Started Now

Time is of the essence.

- The longer you wait, the less time you have in your life for compounding.
- The longer you wait, the more taxes (freedom) the Government will take from your savings.

- The longer you wait, the longer it will take to become fully financially independent.

It's about Money, Choice and Freedom.

Build Your Bunker

www.BuildYourBunker.com/HELP

Recommended Reading

The Pirates of Manhattan II – Barry James Dyke

The Great Deformation: The Corruption of Capitalism in America – David A. Stockman

The Road to Serfdom – F. A. Hayek

The Case Against The Fed – Murray N. Rothbard

How Privatized Banking Really Works – L. Carlos Lara, Robert Murphy, Phd.

The Bastiat Collection – Claude Frederic Bastiat

Becoming Your Own Banker – R. Nelson Nash

Comeback America – David M. Walker

Financial Crisis Inquiry Report –Superintendent of Documents, U.S. Government

Freedom Shift – Oliver DeMille

End The Fed – Ron Paul

Propaganda – Edward Bernays

Creature From Jeckyl Island – G. Edward Griffin

The Great Wall Street Retirement Scam – Rick Bueter

If you have never read these documents in full, please take the time and reaffirm the Freedom the Founders gave their lives for:

The Declaration of Independence

The Constitution of The United States of America

If you know what is going on, you know what to do.

Build Your Bunker.

About The Author

Some call him a visionary: others have said he is an American patriot.

In 1982, Rick Bueter entered the financial planning industry.

He began his training by studying and passing the life insurance agents exam administered by the state department of insurance. After that studied and took exams administered by FINRA (formerly the NASD) to become a stockbroker and salesman of mutual funds. Shortly after, he took correspondence courses from the College for Financial Planning in Denver Colorado to become a Certified Financial Planner in 1985.

Rick is an expert in the area of government taxation of retirement plan assets and the tax code that applies to insurance companies. National Underwriter, a leading publisher of tax information for professionals, has published his research on tax-sheltered assets in the estate. He has also has several publications of his own including The Living Estate Plan For IRAs.

Before the stock market crash in 2009, he knew something was terribly wrong in the financial markets and moved all of his clients out of the markets in 2008 before the crash. In his previous best selling book The Great Wall Street Retirement Scam he writes about that experience and how he was able to see what so many other advisors did not.

Today Rick is retired from Wall Street. He holds only one professional license; that of an insurance agent regulated by the 50 states, not the Federal Government. When you understand that the Federal Government regulates Wall Street and the Banks, and then you look at the track record, it's no wonder that Financial Bunkers come from insurance companies.

After having three years to observe the dynamic changes occurring in America, Rick sees something that everyone concerned about their Freedom needs to prepare for. He sees the Confiscation of Freedom through money.

Rick is a frequent speaker where Americans are gathered who are concerned about their Money and Freedom. He has appeared on talk radio programs across the country sharing his perspective on money, government and freedom. You can listen to Rick on his online radio show Financial Bunker Radio.

For more information and to subscribe to his weekly updates on Money and Freedom visit **www.RickBueter.com.**